Claire Sun-ok Choi *Translated by Yonghyun Kim*

designing handcrafted
CARDS

QUARRY BOOKS

STEP-BY-STEP TECHNIQUES *for* CRAFTING 60 BEAUTIFUL CARDS

paper quilling, decorative cutting, piercing, embossing, folding, layering, weaving, and more!

First published in English by
Quarry Books, an imprint of Rockport Publishers, Inc.
33 Commercial Street
Gloucester, Massachusetts 01930-5089
Telephone: (978) 282-9590
Fax: (978) 283-2742
www.rockpub.com

Library of Congress Cataloging-in-Publication data available upon request.

ISBN 1-59253-036-2

10 9 8 7 6 5

Design: Dongjun Im
Cover Image: Hyuungi Lee and Zangyol Pyo

Printed in Singapore

Introduction

"The time that I enjoy most is when I am with playing with papers of various colors."

It is an exciting and happy experience to receive a card filled with sender's best wishes. Regardless of the complexity of its design, a card with its special meaning and message is a thoughtful gift that touches the heart of the receiver. Receiving a handmade card doubles the pleasure, allowing someone to appreciate both the tender message and artistic endeavor. And it is a pleasure for the card-maker, as well, to create a card while keeping a special person in mind.

New Year's, Valentine's Day, Easter, Mother's day, Father's day, Thanksgiving, and Christmas—all these annual celebrations are wonderful opportunities to express your love and happiness to someone.

These days, we can deliver our thoughts through ready-made cards or email quickly and easily, but somehow, it's not completely fulfilling. In contrast, a handmade card has a special characteristic—it can be preserved and displayed like a piece of artwork or a painting.

The charm of making a card lies in its process—creating a fresh design, using an exquisite combination of colors, enjoying the delicate cutting and folding—that holds our concentration throughout. One of the best ways to create an original card is to use or substitute the materials you already have together with the materials required.

In this book, I intend to show that you can make wonderful cards with just simple tools and colorful papers. After making some of the cards presented here, you may feel inclined to create some original designs on your own. Experiment with creative approaches, discovering exquisite color combinations by leafing through magazines, finding new papers, or strolling by display windows, and crystallize them into a new idea.

I hope that this book guides you in the art of designing handmade cards and helps you expand your aesthetic sensibilities. I want to express my special thanks to designers Dongjun Im and photographers Hyuungi Lee and Zangyol Pyo.

−May 2002, **Claire Sun-ok Choi**

Contents

Tools and Supplies

PATTERNS

Using tracing paper to transfer images and characters onto another paper has long been the most common pattern-making method. However, it can be time-consuming. Many people now find it easier to use a photocopier to reproduce—even reduce or enlarge—images. The copied patterns can then be placed on top of the project paper and used as a cutting guideline.

PAPER

Because paper is a very important material in making cards, use moderately thick, good quality paper that is easy to cut. It is good to use crinkle paper in various colors with moderate thickness and a soft surface that can be hand-torn and works well with punches, craft knives, and scissors.

PUNCH WHEEL

A punch wheel is one of the most useful tools for making the cards in this book. It can be used to transform an even surface into a three-dimensional one. A punch wheel can add elegance to your cards by creating lace-style and stitching borders.

SCISSORS

Generally speaking, there are two types of scissors: those that simply cut and those that cut and add style at the same time. These days, we can easily obtain a variety of decorative scissors: ripple, lace, wave, stamp, sunshine, seagull, bubbles, and so much more. No matter which pair you are looking for, it is important to choose lightweight and comfortable scissors.

ADHESIVE

It is important to choose adhesive suitable for use with paper. PVA adhesive is suitable, because it is permanent, firm, and transparent when it dries. Spray adhesive is good for preventing wrinkles when using thin paper, and it won't cause stains when paper is detached and reattached. However, it can be quite messy, so surrounding table areas should be protected.

TAPE

Foam tape is good for creating a three-dimensional effect on cards. Transparent tape is suitable for the temporary attachment of paper.

AWL AND NEEDLE TOOLS

An awl can be used as a pencil substitute when drawing lines or marking sections to cut. Also, you can use an awl to create lace-style patterns in paper. Quilling needles with grips are perfect for making paper-quilling flowers or for applying small quantities of adhesive.

CUTTING MAT

Use a cutting mat to protect the blades of craft knives and the surface you are working on. Cutting mats prevent papers from curling and can be used as measurement tools instead of rulers because they have horizontal and vertical lines every centimeter.

CRAFT KNIFE

It would be hard to make cards without using a craft knife. It's best to choose a knife that is not shaky, is easy to grip, and has changeable blades. Use a knife at a 45-degree angle to ensure crisp cuts.

TWEEZERS

Many of the cards included in this book require delicate work. Sometimes it is difficult to move tiny pieces with your bare hands. Fine-pointed tweezers can help you handle small paper-quilling shapes.

CORKBOARD

When using an awl or a punch wheel, it's best to work on a $\frac{1}{10}$" (2 mm)-thick corkboard. This allows the awl and punch wheel to function properly.

PUNCHES

Using various types of punches—stars, hearts, flowers, snowflakes, butterflies—will provide you with many design options for your cards. A punch with a variety of shapes to choose from is convenient for all projects.

METAL RULER

Metal rulers are more accurate and safer to use than plastic rulers when cutting papers with a craft knife.

EMBOSSING TOOLS OR PRESS PENS AND TRACING PENS

These tools, with round-tipped metal ends, can be used to press designs into the paper. When they are used from the front of the paper, you are pressing, since the design is pushed into the paper. When they are used from the back of the paper, it's called embossing, since the design appears raised from the front view. Press pens are good for making indented patterns, and tracing pens are good for embossing patterns. Embossing tools can be used for both.

PENS

Gel pens in various colors work well for decorating cards.

GRAPH PAPER AND TRACING PAPER

Graph paper with measurements makes it easy to design shapes. Because tracing paper is soft and transparent, it can create elegant pastel tones when layered over paper. Tracing paper can also make special effects when used for printing computer images.

Techniques

To make a card, we usually purchase one that is partially ready-made at a stationery store or an art shop. However, if you learn basic techniques, such as measuring and cutting, and make one entirely on your own, you can double your satisfaction.

The following sections will help beginners learn how to make the basic shapes of cards. Cards appearing in this book measure 5" x 5" (12.5 cm x 12.5 cm). If it is your first time using craft knives and you have trouble making the shape you want, don't give up. Continue practicing and you will learn the proper way before long.

Basic Card I

This card is a basic 5" (12.5 cm) square card.

① Position the paper on a cutting mat.

② Using a ruler and craft knife, cut a 10" x 5" (25 cm x 12.5 cm) rectangle.

③ Fold the rectangle in half to make a 5" x 5" (12.5 cm x 12.5 cm) square.

Basic Card II

This card opens like a set of doors.

① Follow Step 1 and 2 of Basic Card I to create a rectangle.

② Measure and mark a line 2½" (6.25 cm) in from each short side.

③ Fold along each marked line toward the center, where the edges should meet. Be careful not to make a gap between the two doors on the front cover.

Paper-Quilling

Paper-quilling flowers add a special touch to birthday, wedding, and congratulation cards. Use ¹⁄₁₀" (2 mm)-wide paper ribbon, a paper-quilling needle, paper glue, and scissors. Below are the quilling methods for the shapes used in this book.

TIGHT CIRCLE

Grab one end of paper ribbon with your fingers. With the other hand, rub the paper ribbon with the needle to make the ribbon soft. (Be careful not to make the ribbon curl up.) Coil the ribbon with the needle while your fingers press the ribbon firmly to ensure a tight coil. After coiling the ribbon with the needle two or three times, pull out the needle and carefully roll the ribbon to the end. Glue the end to complete a tight circle.

TEARDROP

Coil paper ribbon into a tight circle, and then loosen the coil, controlling the size with your fingers. Hold the center of the roll with your fingers or tweezers and pinch the opposite side to make a point. Press the opposite side of the roll and glue it with paper adhesive to complete a teardrop.

MARQUISE

Coil paper ribbon into a tight circle, and then loosen the roll to make a loose circle. Pinch opposite points of the circle with your fingers to complete a marquise shape.

APPLICATION

Depending on the length of paper ribbon or the number of petals (one teardrop per petal), you can make flowers of varying sizes. Most flowers can be completed with five or six teardrops placed around a tight circle center. Marquise-shaped quillings can also be used for petals.

MATERIALS

white card stock,
  10" x 5" (25 cm x 12.5 cm)
white paper
graph paper
light box
awl
metal ruler
pencil
transparent tape
cutting mat
craft knife
embossing tool or press pen

BASIC CARDS Pressing

1. With a pencil, mark a 3⅛" x 3⅛" (8 cm x 8 cm) square at the center of 5" x 5" (12.5 cm x 12.5 cm) graph paper.

2. Place the graph paper on 5" x 5" (12.5 cm x 12.5 cm) white paper and use an awl to poke the four corners of the 3⅛" x 3⅛" (8 cm x 8 cm) square through the white paper.

3. Remove the graph paper and make sure the four points appear on the white paper.

4. Use a metal ruler and craft knife to cut out the 3⅛" x 3⅛" (8 cm x 8 cm) square marked by the points on the white paper.

5. Place the frame-shaped paper created in Step 4 on 10" x 5" (25 cm x 12.5 cm) white card stock. Use transparent tape to attach the 3⅛" x 3⅛" (8 cm x 8 cm) square back into the center of the frame. Then, lift the frame; the square should be exactly at the center of the white card stock. Detach the external rectangle 5" x 5" (12.5 cm x 12.5 cm). You should be able to see the inner rectangle exactly at the center of the white card paper.

6. Put the white card stock on a light box. Make a square by using an embossing tool to draw lines two or three times along the lines of the square. When you turn the card stock over, you should see a pressed square border at the center.

MATERIALS

white card stock,
   10" x 5" (25 cm x 12.5 cm)
graph paper
awl
metal ruler
pencil
cutting mat
craft knife

Basic Window-Shaped Card I

1. With a pencil, draw a 3⅕" x 3⅕" (8 cm x 8 cm) square on 5" x 5" (12.5 cm x 12.5 cm) graph paper.

2. Put the graph paper on white card stock and use an awl to poke the four corners of the 3⅕" x 3⅕" (8 cm x 8 cm) square through the card stock.

3. Remove the graph paper and make sure the four points appear on the card stock.

4. Cut out the square using a metal ruler and craft knife.

MATERIALS

white card stock,
  10" x 5" (25 cm x 12.5 cm)
white paper
graph paper
awl
metal ruler
pencil
transparent tape
light box
cutting mat
craft knife
embossing tool or press pen

Basic Window-Shaped Card II

1. With a pencil, draw a 2¼" x 2¼" (6 cm x 6 cm) square on 5" x 5" (12.5 cm x 12.5 cm) graph paper. Mark a smaller 2⅛" x 2⅛" (5.8 cm x 5.8 cm) square within the 2¼" x 2¼" (6 cm x 6 cm) square.

2. Put the graph paper on top of 5" x 5" (12.5 cm x 12.5 cm) white paper and use an awl to poke through the papers at the eight corners of the squares.

3. Remove the graph paper and make sure the eight points appear on the white paper.

4. Use a metal ruler and craft knife to cut out the 2¼" x 2¼" (6 cm x 6 cm) square from the white paper.

5. Spread 10" x 5" (25 cm x 12.5 cm) white card stock on the front side and put the frame-shaped white paper made in Step 5 on the white card stock. Use transparent tape to attach the 2¼" x 2¼" (6 cm x 6 cm) square into the center of the frame and then remove the frame.

6. Place the white card stock on a light box. Make a square by using an embossing tool to draw lines two or three time along the lines of the square. When you turn the card stock over, you should see a square press at the center.

7. Cut out the 2⅛" x 2⅛" (5.8 cm x 5.8 cm) square on the front side of the white card stock.

MATERIALS

white card stock,
  10" x 5" (25 cm x 12.5 cm)
white paper
graph paper
awl
metal ruler
cutting mat
craft knife
transparent tape

Basic Window-Shaped Card III

1. Follow the instructions for Pressing (p. 12) and Basic Window-Shaped Card I (p.13).

2. Design four 1¹⁄₁₀" x 1¹⁄₁₀" (2.8 cm x 2.8 cm) squares on graph paper or use the pattern on page 91.

3. Put the patterns on the front side of the white card stock and use an awl to poke the four corners of each of the four squares through the card stock. Cut out the four squares with a metal ruler and craft knife.

MATERIALS

white card stock,
   10" x 5" (25 cm x 12.5 cm)
white paper,
   5" x 5" (12.5 cm x 12.5 cm)
graph paper
awl
metal ruler
transparent tape
pencil
cutting mat
craft knife

Basic Window-Shaped Card IV

1. Follow the instructions for Basic Window-Shaped Card III (p.15).

2. Design nine 1" x 1" (2.5 cm x 2.5 cm) squares on graph paper with a pencil or use the pattern on page 91. The spaces between the squares should be ⅕" (5 mm).

3. Put the graph paper on the front side of white card stock and use an awl to poke the four corners of each of the squares through the card stock.

4. Remove the graph paper and use a metal ruler and craft knife to cut out the nine squares.

MATERIALS

white card stock,
  10" x 5" (25 cm x 12.5 cm)
white paper,
  4¾" x 2" (12 cm x 5 cm)
flower stencil pattern
light box
pencil
cutting mat
craft knife
embossing tool or press pen

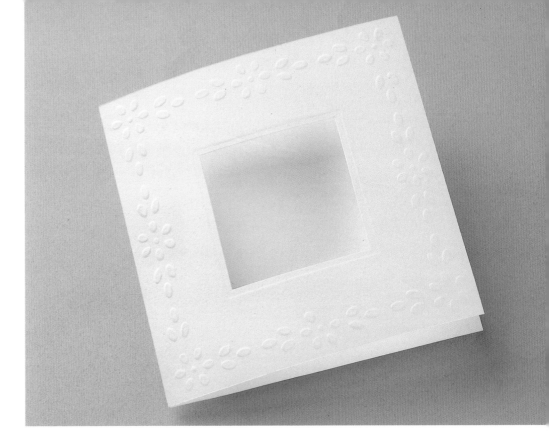

Basic Embossing

1. Use the flower stencil pattern on page 91. Place the pattern on a 4¾" x 2" (12 cm x 5 cm) sheet of white paper and trace the shapes with a pencil. Place the paper on a cutting mat and cut out the flower shapes.

2. Place the flower stencil pattern on a light box and spread the back side of white card stock on it. Rub each flower shape with an embossing tool two or three times so the shapes appear on the card stock. Continue around all four edges to complete the design.

3. Turn the white card stock to the front cover. Follow the instructions from Pressing (p. 12) and Basic Window-Shaped Card I (p.13).

New Year

MATERIALS

white wrinkled card stock,
 10" x 5" (25 cm x 12.5 cm)
jade, brown, taupe, red, pink,
 and orange crinkle paper
thick white paper
graph paper
awl
metal ruler
pencil
PVA adhesive
corkboard
punch wheel
craft knife
heart punch

Traditional Pattern Card I

1. Draw two 2" x 2" (5 cm x 5 cm) squares on graph paper and use an awl to mark the four corners of the squares on the jade and brown crinkle paper.

2. Remove the graph paper and mark a diagonal line with an awl and a metal ruler from one corner to the opposite corner.

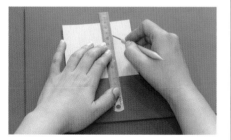

3. Put the jade paper on a corkboard and roll a punch wheel along the edges and along the diagonal line for a stitched appearance.

4. Cut the jade paper in half diagonally to make two triangles. Do the same with the brown paper.

5. Repeat Steps 1 and 2 to make a 1⅕" x 1⅕" (3 cm x 3 cm) square on taupe crinkle

paper. Cut out a ⅖" x ⅖" (2 cm x 2 cm) square window with a craft knife. Attach a red 1" x 1" (2.5 cm x 2.5 cm) square to the back side of the taupe paper.

6. Cut four rounded quarter-circle shapes out of orange paper. Poke the edges of the pieces with an awl for a stitched appearance.

7. Follow Steps 1 through 4 to make a 3⅕"

x 3⅕" (8 cm x 8 cm) square of thick white paper.

8. Attach the four jade and brown triangles to the white square in the shape of a square. The ends of the triangles should overlap. Attach the taupe 1⅕" x 1⅕" (3 cm x 3 cm) square to the center of the triangles and attach the orange quarter-circles to each corner of the brown and jade triangles.

9. Punch a butterfly out of pink paper and attach it to the center of the red square.

10. Use a punch wheel to add a stitched appearance to the overlapped areas of the triangles. Attach the entire square to the white card stock.

MATERIALS

rice card stock,
  10" x 5" (25 cm x 12.5 cm)
thick pale gray paper
white, pale pink, pale red, brown,
  and ocher crinkle paper
graph paper
awl
metal ruler
pencil
small flower punch
corkboard
punch wheel

Traditional Pattern Card II

1. Draw two 1" x 1" (2.5 cm x 2.5 cm) squares on graph paper with a pencil.

2. Place one of the squares on pale red crinkle paper and mark the corners with an awl. Remove the graph paper and cut the square out with a metal ruler and craft knife.

3. Put the pale red crinkle square on a corkboard and roll a punch wheel along the edges to create a stitched appearance.

4. Follow Steps 1 through 3 to make two squares each of white, pale pink, brown, and ocher crinkle paper. You should then have nine squares in total.

5. Make a 3⅕" x 3⅕" (8 cm x 8 cm) square with a thick pale gray paper.

6. Attach the nine small squares to a 2¾" x 2¾" (7 cm x 7 cm) square of graph paper so they are lined up next to each other like quilt squares. (Using graph paper helps ensure the squares are attached straight.)

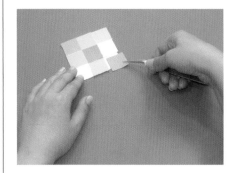

7. Attach the graph paper with the nine squares to the thick pale gray square and add stitching to the edges with a punch wheel.

Punch out five flowers and attach white circles at the center of each flower. Attach the flowers to the center of five of the squares. Adhere the pale gray paper to rice card stock.

MATERIALS

ivory card stock,
   10" x 5" (25 cm x 12.5 cm)
thick ivory paper
jade, orange, beige, brown,
   and red crinkle paper
graph paper
seven khaki paper ribbons,
   ¹⁄₁₀" x 3¹⁄₅" (2 mm x 8 cm)
six orange paper ribbons,
   ¹⁄₁₀" x 9¹⁄₂" (2 mm x 24 cm)
two brown paper ribbons,
   ¹⁄₁₀" x 9¹⁄₂" (2 mm x 24 cm)
pencil
PVA adhesive
cutting mat
craft knife
metal ruler
punch wheel

Traditional Pattern Card III

1. Design a trapezoid ²⁄₅" x 1¹⁄₅" x 3" (2 cm x 3 cm x 7.5 cm) on graph paper or use the pattern on page 92. Stack jade, orange, beige, and brown papers together and use an awl to mark the four corners of the trapezoid.

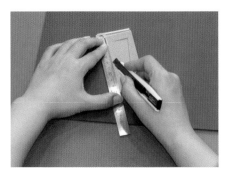

2. Remove the graph paper and cut the trapezoid shape out of all the paper at once.

3. Adhere the four trapezoids to a 2³⁄₄" x 2³⁄₄" (7 cm x 7 cm) piece of thick ivory paper. The trapezoids should form a 3" x

3" (7.5 cm x 7.5 cm) square with a smaller 1" x 1" (2.5 cm x 2.5 cm) square opening in the center.

4. Attach a 1³⁄₅" x 1³⁄₅" (4 cm x 4 cm) square of red paper in the center space.

5. Attach the entire square to the center of ivory card stock.

6. Wind brown and orange paper ribbons around a paper-quilling needle so that the ribbons become long spirals. Attach the spiral ribbons to the long edges of the

trapezoids. Use a small amount of adhesive so the spirals will not unwind.

7. Make a teardrop petal flower using seven khaki paper ribbons and attach it to the red square.

8. Roll a punch wheel along the edges of the ivory card stock and from each corner of the card inward to each corner of the decorative square.

MATERIALS

white card stock,
  10" x 5" (25 cm x 12.5 cm)
purple, lavender, and
  pale blue paper
four white paper ribbons,
  ¹⁄₁₀" x 1¹⁄₅" (2 mm x 3 cm)
awl
yellow highlighter
pencil
flower stamp
ink
corkboard
punch wheel
silver embossing powder
heat gun

Traditional Pattern Card IV

1. Make a basic white card using the instructions for Pressing (p. 12).

2. Use an awl to draw a 2⁷⁄₁₀" x 2⁷⁄₁₀" (5.5 cm x 5.5 cm) square on purple paper and a 1³⁄₅" x 1³⁄₅" (4 cm x 4 cm) square on lavender paper.

3. Put the purple paper on a corkboard and use a punch wheel along the edges to give the appearance of stitching.

4. Tear the purple paper along the awl lines. Tear the marked square out of the lavender paper in the same way.

5. Attach the lavender rectangle to the center of the purple paper with PVA adhesive. Place it on a corkboard and use a punch wheel along the edges for a stitched appearance.

6. Attach the square to the center of the white card stock and attach eight ²⁄₅" x ²⁄₅" (1 cm x 1 cm) pale blue squares to the card stock around the purple square.

7. Stamp a flower at the center of the lavender square. While the ink is still wet, spread silver embossing powder, shake off any excess powder, and then melt it with a heat gun. Paint the flower petals with a yellow highlighter. Use the highlighter to add dots in a flower pattern to each of the blue squares. Make tight circles using white paper ribbon and attach them to the corners of the purple square.

MATERIALS

white card stock,
  10" x 5" (25 cm x 12.5 cm)
taupe rice paper
brown, coral, red, and
  beige crinkle paper
thick pale gray paper
tracing paper
awl
metal ruler
spray adhesive
PVA adhesive
cutting mat
craft knife
corkboard
punch wheel
heart punch

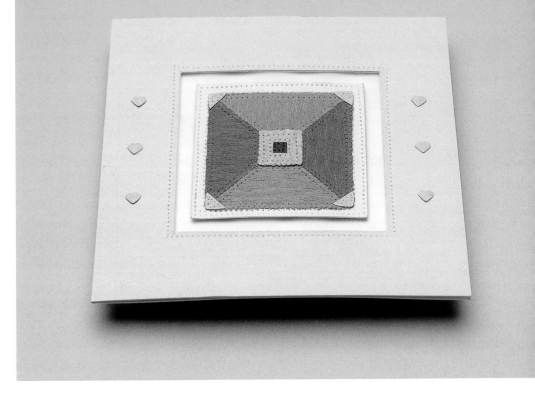

Traditional Pattern Card V

1. Use spray adhesive to attach a 5" x 5" (12.5 cm x 12.5 cm) square of taupe rice paper to one half of the white card stock and proceed to make a Basic Window-Shaped Card (p. 13). Use a punch wheel to add a stitched appearance around the window.

2. Attach tracing paper between the covers as an interior page.

3. Cut a 2¼" x 2¼" (6 cm x 6 cm) square out of thick pale gray paper.

4. Use a craft knife and metal ruler to cut two 1⅖" x 1⅖" (3.5 cm x 3.5 cm) squares out of brown and coral crinkle paper.

5. Place the crinkle paper on a corkboard and use a punch wheel to create a stitched appearance.

6. On the graph paper used to design the 1⅖" x 1⅖" (3.5 cm x 3.5 cm) squares, draw an X from corner to corner to divide the square into four isosceles triangles. Place the graph paper on the brown and coral squares and mark the corners of the triangles with an awl. Use a craft knife and metal ruler to cut out two triangles.

7. Make a ½" x ½" (1.5 cm x 1.5 cm) square of beige crinkle paper with a ⅕" x ⅕" (5 mm x 5 mm) window in the center. Attach a ½" x ½" (1.5 cm x 1.5 cm) square of red crinkle paper behind the beige frame.

8. Adhere the four isosceles triangles to the 2¼" x 2¼" (6 cm x 6 cm) pale gray square so that the same color isosceles triangles face each other. Attach the square from Step 7 to the center of the triangles.

9. Punch four hearts out of beige paper and cut the pieces in half horizontally. Attach the bottom pieces of the hearts to the corners of the square made by the triangles. Poke the pieces with an awl for a stitched appearance.

10. Attach the rectangle to the center of the card stock window and add three beige punched hearts to each side of the window.

Anniversary

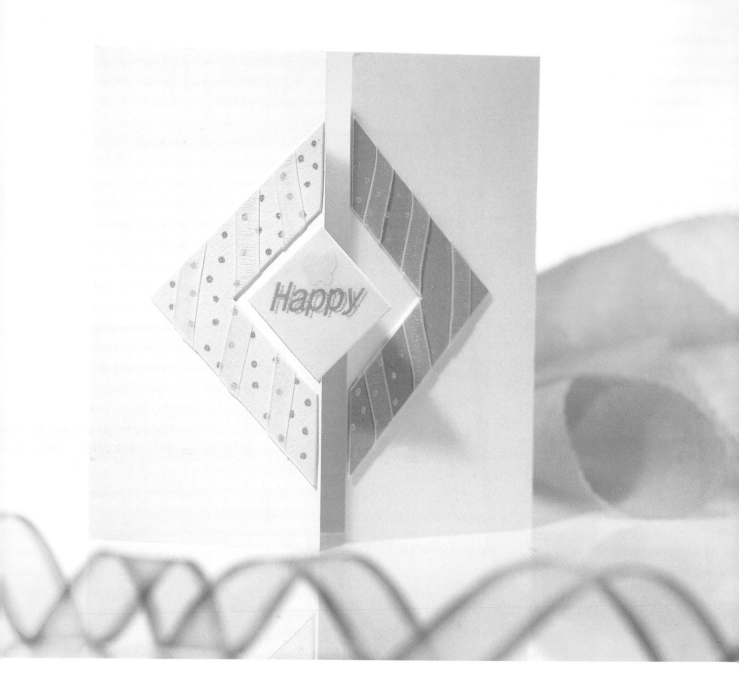

MATERIALS

white card stock,
  10" x 5" (25 cm x 12.5 cm)
thick white, lavender,
  and gray paper
lavender-pearl paper
tracing paper
two translucent white
  ribbons, 8" (20 cm) long
foam tape
metal ruler
butterfly punch
spray adhesive
PVA adhesive
cutting mat
craft knife

Diamond and Lace Ornament

1. Make a door-shaped card using the instructions for Basic Card II (p. 10).

2. Print "Happy" lettering on tracing paper with a computer printer.

3. Cut a 2½" x 2½" (6.5 cm x 6.5 cm) square out of thick white paper. Cut two 2½" x 2½" (6.5 cm x 6.5 cm) squares each out of lavender and gray paper and cut them in half to make triangles. Attach a lavender triangle and a gray triangle to the thick white paper with spray adhesive and cut a 1³⁄₁₀" x 1³⁄₁₀" (3.3 cm x 3.3 cm) window in the center to make a frame shape.

4. Cut the lavender and gray frames diagonally so they form arrows. Use a silver gel pen to draw dots on the arrows and wrap ribbon around both arrows.

5. Cut a 1¹⁄₁₀" x 1¹⁄₁₀" (2.7 cm x 2.7 cm) square out of lavender-pearl paper. Cut a 1¹⁄₁₀" x 1¹⁄₁₀" (2.7 cm x 2.7 cm) diamond around "Happy" on the tracing paper.

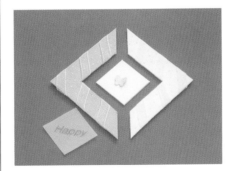

6. Punch out a butterfly and attach it to the lavender-pearl square together with the "Happy" diamond.

7. Attach the square (turned to be a diamond so "Happy" is horizontal) at the center of the white card. Use foam tape to adhere the lavender arrow on the left side of the "Happy" square and the gray arrow on the right side.

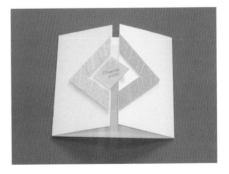

Variation: Make thank-you cards by following the same steps and replace "Happy" with "Thank you."

MATERIALS

blue card stock,
  10" x 5" (25 cm x 12.5 cm)
green, orange, pale green,
  red, and white paper
graph paper
foam tape
metal ruler
multicircle punch
decorative-edge scissors
small flower punch
PVA adhesive
cutting mat
craft knife
tweezers

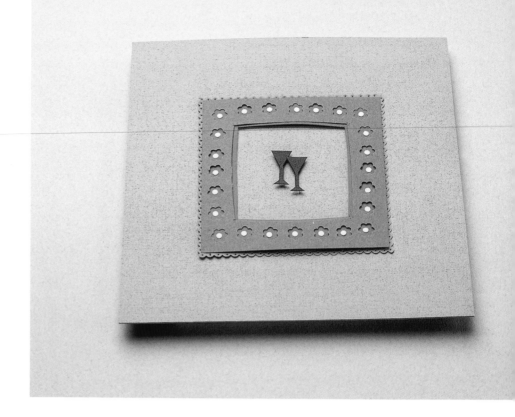

Wine Glasses in a Frame

1. Put a 2¾" x 2¾" (7 cm x 7 cm) green square on a cutting mat and use a craft knife to cut out a 1⅗" x 1⅗"(4 cm x 4 cm) square from the center or use the frame pattern on page 92.

2. Mark six holes on each side of the frame with an awl and punch them with a small flower punch.

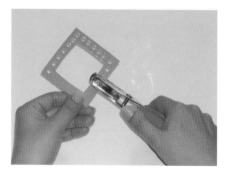

3. Use foam tape to attach a 2⁷⁄₁₀" x 2⁷⁄₁₀" (6.8 cm x 6.8 cm) orange square to the back side of the green frame and place it on a cutting mat. Use a craft knife

to cut out the orange paper that shows in the center of the frame, but leave a ¹⁄₂₀" (1 mm) margin.

4. Make a pale green 3" x 3" (7.5 cm x 7.5 cm) square and attach the frame to the center of it. Trim the outer margin of the pale green square with decorative-edge scissors, leaving a ¹⁄₁₀" (2 mm) margin. Use a craft knife to cut out the center of the pale green square.

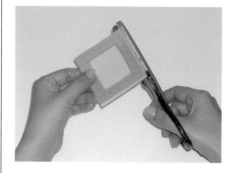

5. Make twenty-four ¹⁄₂₀" (1 mm) circles and use PVA adhesive to attach them to the centers of the flower-shaped holes in the frame.

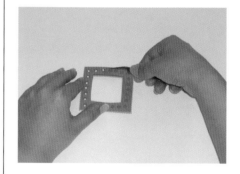

6. Use the pattern on page 92 to cut two wine glasses out of red paper.

7. Use PVA adhesive to attach the frame to the center of the blue card stock and use foam tape to attach the wine glasses in the center of the frame.

MATERIALS

white card stock,
  10" x 5" (25 cm x 12.5 cm)
pale green, lavender, white,
  dark gray, and blue-gray paper
gray-pearl paper
spray adhesive
PVA adhesive
metal ruler
silver and white gel pens
cutting mat
craft knife
small heart punch

Wine Glasses

1. Roughly tear both long edges of a 2¾" x 5⁹⁄₁₀" (7 cm x 15 cm) lavender rectangle. Tear only one side of 2¾" x 5⁹⁄₁₀" (7 cm x 15 cm) pale green and blue-gray rectangles.

2. Use spray adhesive to attach the lavender strip in the middle of white card stock, the pale green strip on the top edge of the card stock, and the blue-gray strip on the bottom edge.

3. Cut a square frame (outer edge 1³⁄₁₀" x 1³⁄₁₀" [3.3 cm x 3.3 cm], inner edge ⁹⁄₁₀" x ⁹⁄₁₀" [2.3 cm x 2.3 cm]) out of dark gray paper and attach a 1³⁄₁₀" x 1³⁄₁₀" (3.3 cm x 3.3 cm) white paper to the back side of it.

4. Use the pattern on page 92 to cut two wine glasses out of white-pearl paper and attach them in the center of the dark gray frame. Attach the frame in the middle of the light purple strip.

5. Use a silver gel pen to make dots on the blue-gray strip and a white gel pen to make dots on the pale green strip.

6. Punch ten hearts out of dark gray paper and attach five each to the blue-gray and the pale green strips.

MATERIALS

white card stock,
  10" x 5" (25 cm x 12.5 cm)
pale gray, pale blue, and
  white paper
awl
small heart punch
spray adhesive
foam tape
PVA adhesive
corkboard
punch wheel
tweezers

Cake and Heart

1. Cut five ⅖" x ⅖" (2 cm x 2 cm) squares out of pale gray paper and seven ⅖" x ⅖" (2 cm x 2 cm) squares out of pale blue paper. (See pattern on page 92.) Roughly tear by hand the edges of all the squares.

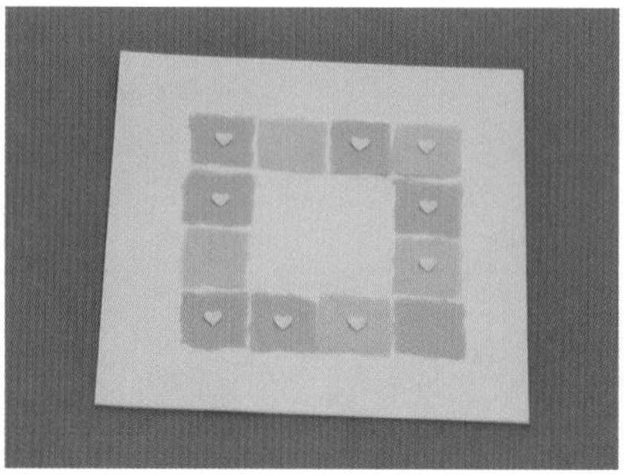

2. Use spray adhesive to attach the squares to white card stock as shown in the picture.

3. Punch nine hearts out of white paper and attach them to the squares.

4. Cut a 1⅗" x 1⅗" (4 cm x 4 cm) square out of white paper, then roughly tear all the edges. Place the square on a corkboard and use a punch wheel to create a stitched appearance. Cut a ⅖" x ⅖" (2 cm x 2 cm) square out of pale blue paper, then tear the edges, and use a punch wheel around the edges. Attach it to the center of the white paper.

5. Cut a three-tiered cake out of white paper and use an awl to create a stitched appearance along the outer edges. (See the pattern on page 92.) Use foam tape to attach the cake to the center of the pale blue square.

6. Attach the white square decorated with the cake to the center of the larger white card stock.

MATERIALS

white card stock,
  10" x 5" (25 cm x 12.5 cm)
lavender and white paper
6 mm circle punch
awl
spray adhesive
foam tape
PVA adhesive
corkboard
white gel pen
embossing tool or press pen
tracing paper
"Anniversary" lettering
  printed on tracing paper with
  a computer printer

Anniversary Cake

1. Punch approximately thirty ²/₁₀" (6 mm) circles out of lavender paper and place them on a corkboard. Add a three-dimensional effect with an embossing tool and attach them to white card stock.

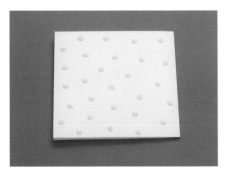

2. Cut a 1⅜" x 1⅜" (4 cm x 4 cm) square out of lavender paper, then roughly tear the edges. Use a white gel pen to make dots on it, and use a punch wheel to create a stitched appearance along the outer edges.

3. Cut a three-tiered cake shape out of white paper and use an awl to create a stitched appearance. (See the pattern on page 92.)

4. Attach the cake shape to the lavender square with foam tape, then attach the square to the center of the white card stock.

5. Adhere the "Anniversary" lettering to the card stock just below the lavender square.

Mother's Day

MATERIALS

white card stock,
  10" x 5" (25 cm x 12.5 cm)
lavender, yellow, pale
  gray-pearl, and white paper
tracing paper
heart and leaf stencil patterns
paper crimper
flower punch
light box
foam tape
metal ruler
cutting mat
craft knife
tracing pen
tweezers

A Flower Vase in a Window

1. Make a card using the instructions for Pressing (p. 12) and Basic Window-Shaped Card I (p.13).

2. Put the heart and leaf stencil patterns on a light box and put the back side of the white window card on it.

3. Center the stencil patterns on one side of the white frame and use a tracing pen to press the pattern into the card. Do the same on the other sides of the frame.

4. Attach a 4¾" x 4¾" (12 cm x 12 cm) tracing paper square to the back side of the 2⁷⁄₁₀" x 2⁷⁄₁₀" (5.5 cm x 5.5 cm) window of the white card.

5. Use a paper crimper to create a corrugated effect on pale gray paper, then cut a flowerpot shape from it. Punch five flower-shaped pieces out of lavender paper. Punch tiny circles out of yellow paper and attach them to the centers of the five flowers.

6. Use a metal ruler and craft knife to cut two thin strips out of white paper. Attach them in a cross shape to the back of the window.

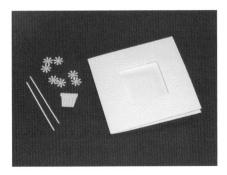

7. Use foam tape to attach the flowerpot to the bottom center of the window. Use tweezers to arrange and adhere the flowers above the flowerpot.

MATERIALS

white card stock,
  10" x 5" (25 cm x 12.5 cm)
white designer's paper
pale red, yellow, green,
  and white crinkle paper
foam tape
awl
metal ruler
decorative-edge scissors
PVA adhesive
cutting mat
craft knife
tweezers

Carnation and Lace Heart

1. Make a card using the instructions for Pressing (p. 12).

2. Use the pattern on page 93 to make a heart-shaped piece of paper, then use a pencil to trace the heart onto the center of the white card stock. Place it on a cutting mat and cut out the heart shape.

3. Place the heart cut out in Step 2 at the center of a 2¾" x 2¾" (7 cm x 7 cm) white square and trace the outer edge with an awl.

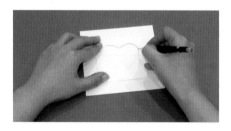

4. Use decorative-edge scissors to cut out the heart just inside the awl line. Poke the center of each rounded section with an awl.

5. Attach the lace heart to the back side of the white card stock and attach a 3⁹⁄₁₀" x 3⁹⁄₁₀" (10 cm x 10 cm) white square behind the lace heart.

6. Using the patterns on page 93, cut three carnations out of red paper. Attach the smaller carnations on top of the bigger carnations. Cut out a calyx and a stem for the flower, attach them to the flower, and attach the entire flower to the center of the heart-shaped space.

7. Make thirteen small rectangles out of yellow paper. Place foam tape on the backs and use tweezers to attach them to the space around the carnation.

8. Print "Happy Mother's Day" lettering on white paper with a computer printer and then cut the strip of paper between "Happy" and "Mother's Day." Tear the edges of the strips of paper and use a punch wheel around the edges of both strips. Attach the words to the card.

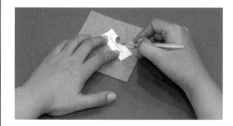

MATERIALS

gray card stock,
  10" x 5" (25 cm x 12.5 cm)
white, lavender, purple, jade,
  and brown paper
foam tape
multicircle punch
decorative-edge scissors
small flower punch
large flower punch
punch wheel
PVA adhesive
tweezers
"Thank you" letters printed
  with a computer printer

Purple Flowers and Flower Vase

1. Make a 2¼" x 2¼" (6 cm x 6 cm) gray card using the instructions for Pressing (p. 12).

2. Cut a 2" x 2" (5 cm x 5 cm) square out of white paper and trim the edge of it with decorative-edge scissors. Use a punch wheel along the outer edges of the square.

3. Use the pattern on page 93 to cut a flowerpot out of brown paper.

4. Make a lavender flower and two purple flowers with a large flower punch. Make three white flowers with a small flower punch and attach them to the larger flowers. Punch three small circles out of yellow paper and attach them to the small white flowers. Make a flower out of jade paper with a large flower punch and cut apart the petals. These will be used as leaves around the flowers.

5. Use tweezers to place and adhere the flowerpot and flowers to the white square. Arrange the jade petal-shaped pieces around the flowers.

6. Attach the white square to the center of the front cover of the gray card stock.

7. Tear the edges of the "Thank You" strip and use a punch wheel or awl along the edges. Attach the strip to the flowerpot.

MATERIALS

pale gray card stock,
  10" x 5" (25 cm x 12.5 cm)
purple, lavender, yellow, pale
  yellow, jade, and white paper
sixteen white paper ribbons,
  ¹⁄₁₀" x 2¼" (2 mm x 6 cm)
three pale yellow paper ribbons,
  ¹⁄₁₀" x 2¼" (2 mm x 6 cm)
scissors
small heart punch
large flower punch
foam tape
transparent tape
PVA adhesive
cutting mat
craft knife
punch wheel
tweezers

A Flower Basket

1. Make a card using the instructions for Basic Window-Shaped Card I (p. 13). The window should measure 2½" x 2½" (6.5 cm x 6.5 cm). Use a punch wheel along the edges of the window.

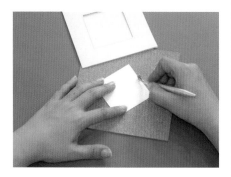

2. Punch out twenty purple hearts and sixteen lavender hearts. Use tweezers to attach four hearts together in a circle to make a flower. Punch nine tiny circles out of yellow paper and attach them to the flower centers.

3. Attach the ends of the white paper ribbons parallel on transparent tape. Interweave the row of white strips with the ends of four white strips and two light yellow strips, alternating the colors. Attach a thick paper at the backside of the interwoven strips for preventing them from being loosened.

4. Trim the excess strips from the woven section to create a basket shape. Attach foam tape on the back side of it, to give it dimension, and attach it to the white square. Arrange the flowers above the basket.

5. Punch two flowers out of jade paper and cut apart the petals to be used as leaves around the flowers.

6. Use a punch wheel along the edges of the white 2¼" x 2¼" (6 cm x 6 cm) square and then attach the square to the interior paper with foam tape.

Valentine's Day

MATERIALS

white card stock,
  10" x 5" (25 cm x 12.5 cm)
eighteen papers in various colors
silver paper
foam tape
metal ruler
spray adhesive
cutting mat
craft knife
large heart punch

Rectangle and Heart

1. Make a card using the instructions for Pressing (p. 12).

2. Categorize the various colored papers into darker-tone and lighter-tone groups and attach the papers in each category together with a stapler. Use a metal ruler and craft knife to cut nine 1" x 1" (2.5 cm x 2.5 cm) squares out of the darker-tone papers and nine ½" x ½" (1.5 cm x 1.5 cm) squares out of the lighter-tone papers.

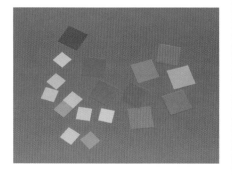

3. Place the nine lighter-tone squares on corrugated cardboard and apply spray adhesive to them.

4. Attach the smaller squares to the larger squares.

5. Punch or cut nine hearts out of silver paper.

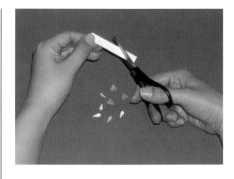

6. Attach the hearts to the center of each square.

7. Use foam tape to attach the nine squares to the white card stock.

MATERIALS

white card stock,
  10" x 5" (25 cm x 12.5 cm)
red and silver paper
decorative-edge scissors
foam tape
silver gel pen
PVA adhesive
cutting mat
craft knife
awl or pencil

Lace and Silver Heart

1. Make a card using the instructions for Basic Window-Shaped Card I (p. 13).

2. Use an awl or pencil to mark lines for a 3⅕" x 3⅕" (8 cm x 8 cm) inner square on a 4¾" x 4¾" (12 cm x 12 cm) sheet of red paper.

3. Mark four strips ½" x 3⁹⁄₁₀" (1.5 cm x 10 cm) on the back side of silver paper and cut the strips out with decorative-edge scissors.

4. Attach the strips with PVA adhesive along the marked lines of the inner square on the red paper.

5. Cut a 1⅕" x 8" (3 cm x 20 cm) strip of silver paper and mark a vertical line down the center of it with an awl. Fold the strip along the awl line and design small and large half heart shapes on it to make ten hearts when unfolded.

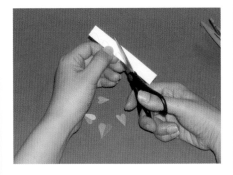

6. Write "I," "LOVE," and "YOU" on the smaller hearts by poking them with an awl and attach them to the larger hearts with foam tape.

7. Attach the red paper to the inside of the white card stock and attach the five hearts to the red square with foam tape. Use a silver gel pen to draw dots around each heart.

MATERIALS

dark blue card stock,
   10" x 5" (25 cm x 12.5 cm)
white, red, and gold paper
PVA adhesive
scissors
awl
metal ruler
craft knife
foam tape
tweezers
embossing tool or press pen

Red Heart

1. Cut out one red 3" x 3" (7.5 cm x 7.5 cm) square and one white 2¾" x 2¾" (7 cm x 7 cm) square.

2. Use an embossing tool to create sixteen small circles in a grid pattern on the back side of the white square. When turned over, the circles should be slightly raised.

3. Cut a heart out of a red 2" x 2" (5 cm x 5 cm) sheet of red paper and poke around the edges with an awl.

4. Use foam tape to attach the red heart to silver paper. Trim the silver paper around the heart, leaving a ¹⁄₂₀" (1 mm) margin of silver.

5. Attach the white square to the red square and attach the heart to the center of the white square.

6. Adhere the red square to the center of the dark blue card stock.

MATERIALS

white card stock,
  10" x 5" (25 cm x 12.5 cm)
red and silver paper
scissors
foam tape
awl
metal ruler
PVA adhesive
cutting mat
craft knife
corkboard
punch wheel
tweezers

Silver and Red Heart

1. Make a card using the instructions for Basic Card II (p. 10).

2. Place the card on corkboard and roll a punch wheel horizontally across the card to add approximately ten wavy lines.

3. Use an awl to mark a vertical line down the center of a 3½" x 2" (8 cm x 5 cm) sheet of red paper. Fold the paper along the line and design a half heart shape on it with a pencil. Cut the heart out. Do the same with a 3½" x 2" (8 cm x 5 cm) sheet of silver paper. (See the pattern on page 93.)

4. Put the hearts on corkboard and poke the outer edges with an awl.

5. Attach foam tape on the back side of the red heart and attach it to the silver heart, allowing some of the silver heart to be seen.

6. Use a craft knife to cut "I," "LOVE," and "YOU" letters out of silver paper.

7. Attach the heart to the left flap of the white card with foam tape. (The right side of the heart should overlap the right flap of the card.) Attach "I," "LOVE," and "YOU" characters to the white card stock with PVA adhesive.

Invitation

MATERIALS

white card stock,
  10" x 5" (25 cm x 12.5 cm)
tan, pale pink, green,
  and gray paper
small butterfly punch
circle punch
foam tape
multicircle punch
awl
metal ruler
scissors
PVA adhesive
corkboard
punch wheel

Flowers and a Butterfly

1. Use an awl and a metal ruler to mark a 2½" x 2½" (6.5 cm x 6.5 cm) square at the center of gray paper and a 2¼" x 2¼" (6 cm x 6 cm) square at the center of tan paper.

2. Place them on a corkboard and roll a punch wheel along the inside edges of the squares to create a stitched appearance.

3. Fold the paper along the marked lines and tear off the margins by hand.

4. Fold a pale pink paper in half twice and punch out four circles. Trim each circle into a petal shape.

5. Attach four petal-shaped pieces together to make a flower and attach a yellow circle at the center of the flower. Make six more flowers in this way.

6. Cut leaf-shaped pieces out of green paper and punch a butterfly out of gray paper.

7. Layer the tan square onto the gray square and attach them both to the card stock with foam tape.

8. Attach the flowers, leaves, and butterflies to the tan square with foam tape.

9. Punch out four small circles and attach them to the four corners of the tan square.

MATERIALS

white card stock,
  10" x 5" (25 cm x 12.5 cm)
jade crinkle paper
red, gray, and white paper
wave-edge scissors
foam tape
metal ruler
small butterfly punch
PVA adhesive
cutting mat
craft knife
tweezers

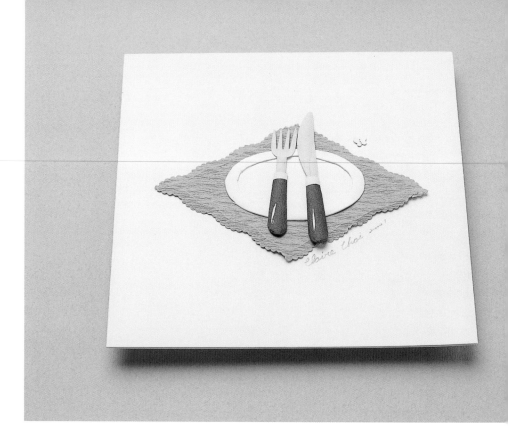

Fork and Knife

1. Design a 3⁹⁄₁₀" x 2¼" (10 cm x 6 cm) diamond shape (or use the pattern on page 93) with a pencil on jade crinkle paper and cut it out with a wave-edge scissors. Mark lines just inside the edge of the diamond with an awl and make a slight fold to add a three-dimensional effect.

2. Copy the fork and knife patterns and attach the tops to gray paper and the handles to red paper.

3. Use a craft knife to delicately cut out the fork and knife shapes.

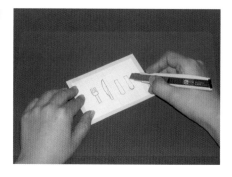

4. Add a three-dimensional effect to the fork and knife by slightly curling them with an awl.

5. Attach the tops and bottoms of the fork and knife together.

6. Make a dish-shaped piece out of white paper and add a three-dimensional effect by slightly curling it with an awl.

7. Use foam tape to attach the diamond at the center of the white card stock and use PVA adhesive to attach the dish to the diamond. Attach the fork and knife to the dish. Punch a small butterfly out of white paper and attach it to the white card stock.

MATERIALS

white card stock,
  10" x 5" (25 cm x 12.5 cm)
red crinkle paper
white, pale green,
  and orange paper
wave-edge scissors
foam tape
awl
metal ruler
PVA adhesive
cutting mat
craft knife

A Red Roof

1. Use the pattern on page 94 to design a roof (a 1⅗" x 1¹⁄₁₀" [4 cm x 2.7 cm] isosceles triangle) and a wall (a 1⅕" x ⁹⁄₁₀" [3 cm x 2.3 cm] rectangle) on graph paper, allowing ⅖" (1 cm) for attaching the pieces together.

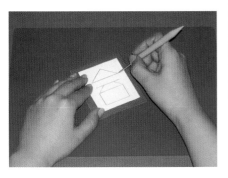

2. Put the roof on red crinkle paper, trace it with an awl, and cut the shape out. Cut out a white wall the same way, being careful when cutting out the windows.

3. Attach the roof and wall together with foam tape and adhere the house to white card stock.

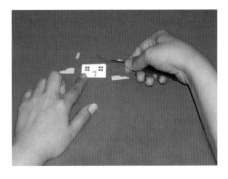

4. Cut a 3" (7.5 cm)-long shrubbery-shaped piece out of pale green paper with wave-edge scissors and cut it in half. Attach one piece of shrubbery to each side of the house. Make a chimney-shaped piece out of orange paper and attach it to the roof.

MATERIALS

pale gray card stock,
  10" x 5" (25 cm x 12.5 cm)
khaki crinkle paper
white, pale gray,
  and pale blue paper
graph paper
wave-edge scissor
multicircle punch
foam tape
awl
metal ruler
pencil
cutting mat
craft knife
PVA adhesive
tweezers

A Coffee Mug

1. Use the pattern on page 94 to design a coffee mug, saucer, and handle on graph paper. Place it on pale gray paper and trace the pattern with an awl.

2. Place the gray paper on a cutting mat and cut out the shapes with a craft knife.

3. Add a three-dimensional effect to the mug, saucer, and handle by slightly curling them with an awl. Attach them together with foam tape.

4. Cut a 2⁷⁄₁₀" x 2⁷⁄₁₀" (5.5 cm x 5.5 cm) square out of khaki crinkle paper with wave-edge scissors. On the back side, use an awl to mark lines ¹⁄₁₀" (2 mm) inside the edges and fold the edges slightly.

5. Attach the khaki square to the center of white card stock with foam tape, then attach the saucer and coffee mug to the center of the khaki square.

6. Attach four small white circles to the four corners of the khaki square. Cut out small wavy pieces to act as steam rising from the mug.

MATERIALS

white card stock,
  10" x 5" (25 cm x 12.5 cm)
dark gray, lavender, green,
  pale green, yellow, pale
  yellow, and white paper
foam tape
small flower punch
awl
metal ruler
PVA adhesive
cutting mat
craft knife
tweezers

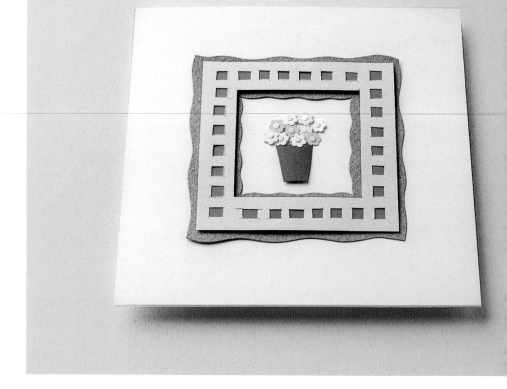

Flowers in a Frame

1. Place a lavender 3" x 3" (7.5 cm x 7.5 cm) square on a cutting mat and cut out a 1⅘" x 1⅘" (4.5 cm x 4.5 cm) square from the center to make a frame. (See the pattern on page 94.)

2. Use an awl to mark eight ⅕" x ⅕" (5 mm x 5 mm) squares on each side of the frame and cut out the small squares.

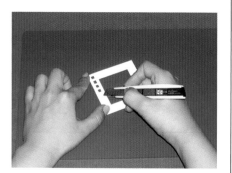

3. Use foam tape to attach the frame to a pale green 2⁹⁄₁₀" x 2⁹⁄₁₀" (7.3 cm x 7.3 cm) square. Place it on a cutting mat and cut out the pale green paper that shows through the frame's window.

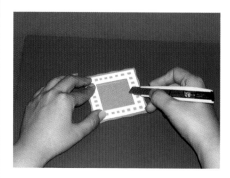

4. Attach the frame to the center of a dark gray 3³⁄₁₀" x 3³⁄₁₀" (8.5 cm x 8.5 cm) square and trim the inner and outer edges of the dark gray square into wavy lines.

5. Make three yellow, four pale yellow, and three white flowers with a small flower punch and attach small pale yellow

circles to the centers of the flowers with tweezers. Cut a flowerpot shape out of green paper and curl it slightly with an awl to add a three-dimensional effect.

6. Use PVA adhesive to attach the frame to the center of white card stock, and use foam tape to attach the flowers and flowerpot in the center of the frame.

MATERIALS

white card stock,
  10" x 5" (25 cm x 12.5 cm)
white paper
flower stencil pattern
light box
transparent tape
cutting mat
craft knife
tracing pen

Embossed Flowers and Happy Birthday

1. Copy the "Happy Birthday" lettering from the pattern on page 94 and attach them to a white 5" x 5" (12.5 cm x 12.5 cm) square. Cut out the characters with a craft knife.

2. Place the "Happy Birthday" lettering backwards on a light box and center white card stock on top.

3. Trace the letters with a tracing pen several times to ensure that the characters appear on the surface of the white card stock.

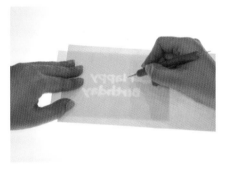

4. Use the same technique to transfer the flower pattern on page 91 to the card stock.

MATERIALS

white card stock,
  10" x 5" (25 cm x 12.5 cm)
pale green, white, yellow,
  and jade paper
scissors
circle punch
spray adhesive
PVA adhesive
metal ruler
craft knife
punch wheel
tweezers

White Flowers and Circles

1. Print "Happy Birthday" lettering on a ⅖" x 2¼" (1 cm x 6 cm) sheet of jade paper.

2. Fold pale green paper in half and punch it thirty times with a circle punch for a total of sixty ⅕" (6 mm) circles. Attach the circles on the front cover of white card stock with PVA adhesive.

3. Use the pattern on page 94 to make two white flowers with yellow centers.

4. Cut a 1⅕" x 5" (3 cm x 12.5 cm) rectangle out of the jade paper around "Happy Birthday" and use a punch wheel along the edges.

5. Attach the rectangle across the center of the white card stock and attach one flower to each end of "Happy Birthday."

MATERIALS

green card stock,
   10" x 5" (25 cm x 12.5 cm)
pale jade and lavender paper
tracing paper
scissors
circle punch
PVA adhesive
stapler
pencil
spray adhesive

Card Embellished with Flowers

1. Print "Happy Birthday" lettering ⅖" x 2¼" (1 cm x 6 cm) on tracing paper with a computer printer.

2. Attach the two flower patterns on page 94 to a stack of three pale jade sheets of paper and cut out six flowers with a scissor by cutting twice.

3. Punch six small circles out of lavender paper and attach them to the centers of the flowers.

4. Use spray adhesive to attach "Happy Birthday" to the center of green card stock.

5. Adhere the flowers to the card stock around the words.

MATERIALS

lavender card stock,
  10" x 5" (25 cm x 12.5 cm)
thick white paper
lavender paper
tracing paper
butterfly punch
metal ruler
silver gel pen
PVA adhesive
cutting mat
craft knife
spray adhesive

A Butterfly and A Frame I

1. Make a card using the instructions for Basic Card II (p. 10).

2. Print "Happy Birthday" lettering on tracing paper with a computer printer and cut it onto a 1⅗" x 3⁹/₁₀" (4 cm x 10 cm) rectangle.

3. Attach lavender paper to thick white paper and cut it to make a 2½" x 2½" (6.5 cm x 6.5 cm) square. Cut out a 1⅕" x 1⅕" (3 cm x 3 cm) inner square at the center.

4. Use a silver gel pen to make dots on the frame and attach the "Happy Birthday" rectangle across the center of the frame with spray adhesive, trimming the excess tracing paper.

5. Cut out a white 1" x 1" (2.5 cm x 2.5 cm) square and attach it to the back side of the characters. Punch out a butterfly and attach it below "Happy Birthday."

6. Attach the left half of the frame to the left flap of the card with PVA adhesive.

Wedding

MATERIALS

white card stock,
  10" x 7⅒" (25 cm x 18 cm)
four white, pale green,
  and ivory paper ribbons
  ⅕" x 5½" (6 mm x 14 cm)
twenty-four white paper ribbons,
  ⅒" x 4¾" (2 mm x 12 cm)
four pale green paper ribbons,
  ⅒" x 2" (2 mm x 5 cm)
scissors
paper-quilling needle
flower-shaped beads
foam tape
silver gel pen
PVA adhesive
cutting mat
craft knife
tracing pen
tweezers

Wedding Card

1. Place the white card stock on a cutting mat with the front side up. Put an oval pattern in the center of it and mark it with a tracing pen. Cut out the oval center. (See the pattern on page 95.)

2. Attach a 4⅘" x 6⁹⁄₁₀" (12.3 cm x 17.5 cm) white rectangle to the back side of the front cover with PVA adhesive.

3. Make a cross with two ivory paper ribbons and attach it to the center of the card.

4. Fold in half two 5½" (9 cm) ivory paper ribbons. Attach both of these folded strips to the center of the cross in the shape of an X.

5. Make twenty-four teardrop quilling pieces using white paper ribbon. Assemble six teardrop pieces to make a flower (four flowers total). Make four tight circles using four pale green paper ribbons and attach them to the centers of the flowers.

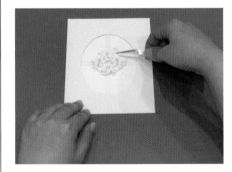

6. Attach the flowers to the X-shaped ribbons with foam tape. Cut leaves out of light green paper and attach them around the flowers.

7. Place pale green paper on foam tape and cut various rectangles with scissors. Use tweezers to arrange them around the flowers.

8. Paint PVA adhesive along the edge of the oval. When adhesive dries, attach flower-shaped beads along the edge.

MATERIALS

white card stock,
  10" x 5" (25 cm x 12.5 cm)
jade paper
thirteen white paper ribbons,
  1/10" x 2 3/4" (2 mm x 7 cm)
thirteen pale green paper ribbons
  1/10" x 2 3/4" (2 mm x 7 cm)
metal ruler
PVA adhesive
cutting mat
craft knife
tweezers

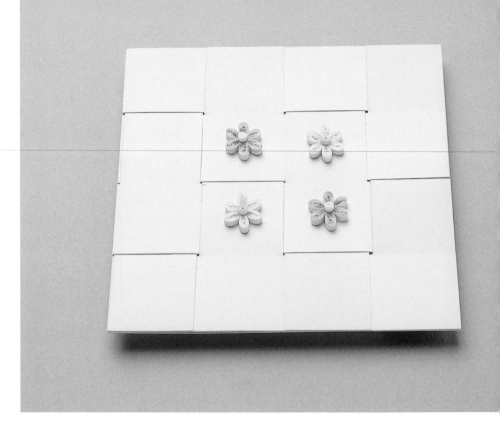

Cross Strips and Paper-Quilling Flowers

1. Place white card stock on a cutting mat and cut the front cover into four even rectangular sections. Trim the rectangles 1/20" (1 mm) more so there is room for weaving.

2. Cut four 1 1/5" x 5" (3 cm x 12.5 cm) strips out of jade paper.

3. Weave the jade strips with the white card stock.

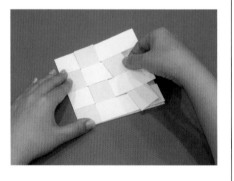

4. Glue the woven strips together with PVA adhesive.

5. Make four teardrop petal flowers using twelve white paper ribbons and twelve pale green paper ribbons. Make four tight circles with white paper ribbon and attach them to the centers of the flowers.

6. Attach the flowers to four woven squares on the card.

MATERIALS

white card stock,
   10" x 5" (25 cm x 12.5 cm)
white and white-pearl paper
twenty-four white paper ribbons,
   1⁄10" x 5 1⁄2" (2 mm x 9 cm)
four pale green paper ribbons,
   1⁄10" x 2" (2 mm x 5 cm)
two ivory paper ribbons,
   1⁄10" x 5 9⁄10" (2 mm x 15 cm)
scissors
foam tape
awl
multicircle punch
metal ruler
decorative-edge scissors
PVA adhesive
cutting mat
craft knife
tweezers

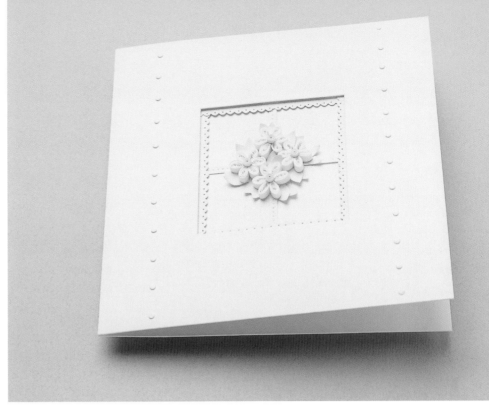

A White Flower on Lace

1. Make a card using the instructions for Pressing (p. 12) and Basic Window-Shaped Card II (p. 14).

2. Cut a white 2 3⁄4" x 2 3⁄4" (7 cm x 7 cm) square and mark a smaller 2 7⁄10" x 2 7⁄10" (5.5 cm x 5.5 cm) square at the center of the white square with an awl.

3. Cut out the inner square with decorative-edge scissors, leaving a 1⁄10" (2 mm) margin. Poke the lace-shaped edges with an awl for embellishment.

4. Attach the lace frame to the back side of the white card stock. Attach a 3 9⁄10" x 3 9⁄10" (10 cm x 10 cm) white-pearl square to the back side of the lace frame. Use a punch wheel in the center of two ivory paper ribbons and position a cross shape at the center of the frame. Attach the ribbons to the back of the window.

5. Make four teardrop petal flowers with white paper ribbons. Make tight circles with pale green paper ribbons and attach them to the centers of the flowers.

6. Use foam tape to attach the four flowers to the center of the ribbon cross. Cut leaves out of white paper and attach them around the flowers.

7. Punch approximately twenty-two 1⁄10" (2 mm) circles out of white paper and attach them in a vertical line on the left and right sides.

MATERIALS

ivory card stock with
  embellished surface,
  10" x 5" (25 cm x 12.5 cm)
pale pink, pink, white,
  and yellow paper
scissors
foam tape
multicircle punch
awl
metal ruler
small flower punch
butterfly punch
PVA adhesive
cutting mat
craft knife
corkboard
large flower punch
punch wheel

A Ribbon and a Garland

1. Make a card using the instructions for Basic Window-Shaped Card I (p. 13).

2. Punch out five large pale pink flowers and five large pink flowers and mark lines between each with an awl. Curl the six petals of each flower with an awl to add a three-dimensional effect.

3. Punch out ten small flowers and attach them to the centers of the larger flowers. Punch out ten small circles and attach the circles to the centers of the small flowers.

4. Use an awl to mark a 1⅗" (4 cm) circle on a white 3⁹⁄₁₀" x 3⁹⁄₁₀" (10 cm x 10 cm) square. Then mark ten points on the circles where the flowers will be attached to form the wreath.

5. Use a punch wheel along the edges of the white square.

6. Attach the flowers with PVA adhesive and tweezers. (See the pattern on page 95 for arrangement.)

7. Use the pattern on page 95 to make a ribbon. Curl it slightly with an awl to add a three-dimensional effect. Attach the ribbon to the top of the wreath.

8. Punch a butterfly out of yellow paper and attach it in the center of the wreath.

9. Attach the white square with the wreath to the white card stock.

MATERIALS

white card stock,
  10" x 5" (25 cm x 12.5 cm)
pale blue, lavender, pale green,
  dark green, red, and silver paper
pale red paper ribbon,
  ³⁄₁₀" x 2" (8 mm x 5 cm)
two white paper ribbons,
  ¹⁄₁₀" x 10³⁄₅" (2 mm x 27 cm)
paper-quilling needle
foam tape
metal ruler
star punch
multicircle punch
spray adhesive
PVA adhesive
cutting mat
craft knife
tweezers

A Christmas Tree and a Star

1. Tear one side of each of a 1³⁄₅" x 5" (4 cm x 12.5 cm) pale blue rectangle and a 1³⁄₅" x 5" (4 cm x 12.5 cm) jade rectangle. Tear both sides of a 1³⁄₅" x 5" (4 cm x 12.5 cm) lavender rectangle. Attach the lavender strip across the center of white card stock with spray adhesive, followed by the pale blue rectangle across the top and the jade rectangle across the bottom.

2. Use the pattern on page 95 to cut a Christmas tree out of dark green paper. Punch out a silver star.

3. Coil under both ends of a pale red

paper ribbon to make a pot. Wind four white paper ribbons around a paper-quilling needle to make spiral garlands.

4. Attach the Christmas tree to the center of the white card stock with foam tape. Attach the spiral ribbons to the Christmas tree with PVA adhesive.

5. Punch out seven red circles and attach them to the Christmas tree.

6. Use foam tape to attach the silver star to the top of the tree and attach the red flowerpot to the foot of the tree.

MATERIALS

white card stock,
  10" x 5" (25 cm x 12.5 cm)
white paper
tracing paper
PVA adhesive
metal ruler
silver gel pen
cutting mat
craft knife
tweezers

A Christmas Tree Covered by Snow

1. Make a card using the instructions for Pressing (p. 12) to make a 2" x 2" (5 cm x 5 cm) square and the instructions for Basic Window-Shaped Card I (p. 13) to make a 1⅕" x 1⅕" (4.5 cm x 4.5 cm) square window.

2. Reduce the Christmas tree pattern on page 95 by 50% and cut the shape out of white paper.

3. Attach a 2" x 2" (5 cm x 5 cm) square of tracing paper behind the front cover and embellish it by dotting with a silver gel pen.

4. Attach a 2" (5 cm)-long paper ribbon vertically through the center of the window and attach the Christmas tree to the ribbon.

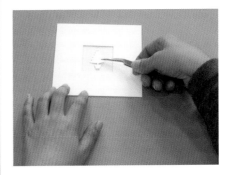

5. Use a silver gel pen to write "Merry Christmas" above the window and your signature below it.

MATERIALS

white card stock,
  10" x 5" (25 cm x 12.5 cm)
red, orange, yellow, green, pale
  green, lavender, blue, dark
  blue, purple, and silver paper
tree punch
foam tape
metal ruler
cutting mat
craft knife
tweezers

Christmas Trees

1. Make a card using the instructions for Pressing (p. 12) to make a 2" x 2" (5 cm x 5 cm) square and the instructions for Basic Window-Shaped Card I (p. 13) to make a 1⅕" x 1⅕" (4.5 cm x 4.5 cm) square window.

2. Cut one tree each out of red, orange, yellow, green, pale green, lavender, blue, dark blue, and purple paper (nine trees in total).

3. Cut out a silver 2¾" x 2¾" (7 cm x 7 cm) square and attach it to the back side of the front cover with foam tape.

4. Use foam tape and tweezers to attach the nine trees in a grid pattern to the silver square.

MATERIALS

red card stock,
  10" x 5" (25 cm x 12.5 cm)
silver, gold, green, red,
  and white paper
scissors
metal ruler
multicircle punch
small circle punch
paper-quilling needle
PVA adhesive
cutting mat
craft knife
punch wheel
tweezers

Poinsettia

1. Cut a 2¼" x 2¼" (6 cm x 6 cm) square out of silver paper with decorative-edge scissors.

2. Cut a 1⅗" x 1⅗" (4 cm x 4 cm) square out of gold paper.

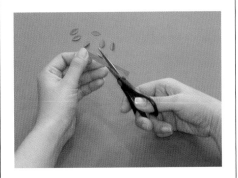

3. Fold red paper in half and draw five half poinsettia petals on it. Do the same with green paper and cut out all the petals.

4. Use PVA adhesive to attach the five green flower petals in a circle arrangement. Attach the five red petals between the green petals.

5. Attach the gold square to the silver square and then the silver square to the center of the red card stock.

6. Punch out three ⅒" (2 mm) green circles and attach them to the center of the poinsettia. Wind two thin, white paper ribbons around a paper-quilling needle and attach them to the poinsettia.

Love

MATERIALS

ivory card stock with
  embellished surface,
  10" x 5" (25 cm x 12.5 cm)
three purple paper ribbons,
  ¹⁄₁₀" x 2 " (2 mm x 5 cm)
pink-purple, blue-purple, pale
  green, yellow, and white paper
scissors
large flower punch
multicircle punch
butterfly punch
foam tape
PVA adhesive
¹⁄₅" (6 mm) circle punch
cutting mat
craft knife
corkboard
punch wheel
tweezers

Purple Flower Garland

1. Make a card using the instructions for Basic Window-Shaped Card I (p.13) to make a 2½" x 2½" (6.5 cm x 6.5 cm) square out of ivory paper with embellished surface and use a punch wheel along the edges of the window.

2. Punch thirty ¹⁄₅" (6 mm) circles out of pink-purple and blue-purple papers and twelve ¹⁄₁₀" (2 mm) circles out of yellow paper.

3. Attach four ¹⁄₅" (6 mm) circles in a circle with tweezers to make six pink-purple flowers and six blue-purple flowers.

Attach the yellow circles to the centers of the flowers.

4. Punch two flowers out of pale green paper and cut apart the petals to be used as leaves.

5. Using the photo for reference, take a strip of purple paper and fold each end into the center to make a ribbon shape. Make another ribbon shape and stack the two ribbons together. Bind them with a strip of paper across the center. Trim the extending ends into a fish tail shape. (See the pattern on page 95.)

6. Mark a 1³⁄₅" (4 cm) circle guideline on a white 3⁹⁄₁₀" x 3⁹⁄₁₀" (10 cm x 10 cm) square and use foam tape to attach the twelve pink-purple flowers and the twelve blue-purple flowers along the circular line.

7. Attach the ribbon to the top of the flower garland. Punch two butterflies out of yellow paper and attach them in the center of the wreath.

8. Attach the white rectangle with the wreath to the window on the back side of the cover.

MATERIALS

white card stock,
  10" x 5" (25 cm x 12.5 cm)
lavender and pale blue paper
twelve pale blue paper ribbons,
  $\frac{1}{10}$" x 2$\frac{3}{4}$" (2 mm x 7 cm)
twelve lavender paper ribbons,
  $\frac{1}{10}$" x 2$\frac{3}{4}$" (2 mm x 7 cm)
four white paper ribbons,
  $\frac{1}{10}$" x 2" (2 mm x 5 cm)
tracing paper
graph paper
metal ruler
spray adhesive
transparent tape
PVA adhesive
cutting mat
craft knife
tweezers

Window and Paper-Quilling Flowers

1. Make a card using the instructions for Basic Window Shape III (p. 15) and attach a tracing paper square behind the front cover. (See the pattern on page 91.)

2. Make four paper-quilling teardrop petal flowers using twelve lavender paper ribbons, twelve pale blue paper ribbons, and four white paper ribbons.

3. Design a 1$\frac{2}{5}$" x 1$\frac{2}{5}$" (3.5 cm x 3.5 cm) square on graph paper. Put it on lavender paper and trace it twice with an awl to make two squares. Do the same on pale blue paper.

4. Attach the four squares together with transparent tape to make a 2$\frac{3}{4}$" x 2$\frac{3}{4}$" (7 cm x 7 cm) square. Attach it to an interior paper with spray adhesive. (To attach it accurately, use a light box.)

5. Use tweezers to attach the teardrop flowers to the center of each coordinating colored square.

MATERIALS

white card stock,
  10" x 5" (25 cm x 12.5 cm)
nine pieces of various
  colored paper
six paper ribbons of nine
  various colors,
  1/10" x 2¾" (2 mm x 7 cm)
nine white paper ribbons,
  1/10" x 2¾" (2 mm x 7 cm)
paper-quilling needle
metal ruler
spray adhesive
PVA adhesive
cutting mat
craft knife
tracing paper
tweezers

Beautiful Paper-Quilling Flowers

1. Make a card using the instructions for Basic Window-Shaped Card IV (p. 16) and attach a 4⁹/₁₀" x 4⁹/₁₀" (12.3 cm x 12.3 cm) square of tracing paper behind the front cover. (See the pattern on page 96.)

2. Make one 1" x 1" (2.5 cm x 2.5 cm) square out of each shade of paper, totaling nine squares.

3. Put the nine squares on corrugated cardboard and apply spray adhesive.

4. Use tweezers to attach each of the nine squares to tracing paper in a grid pattern.

5. Make nine marquise petal flowers using each color of paper ribbon. (Each flower should have six same-color petals.) Make nine tight circles using white paper ribbon and attach them to the centers of the flowers.

6. Attach one flower to the center of each square.

MATERIALS

white card stock,
  10" x 5" (25 cm x 12.5 cm)
lavender, gray, yellow, dark jade,
  white, and pale blue paper
white corrugated board
flower punch
circle punch
metal ruler
multicircle punch
decorative-edge scissors
PVA adhesive
cutting mat
craft knife
spray adhesive

Flowers on Corrugated Cardboard

1. Cut four 2½" x 2½" (6.25 cm x 6.25 cm) squares out of lavender, gray, yellow, and dark jade paper and attach them to white card stock with spray adhesive.

2. Cut a 2" x 2" (5 cm x 5 cm) square out of white corrugated paper and attach it to white paper. Trim the edges of the white square with decorative-edge scissors to add a lace embellishment.

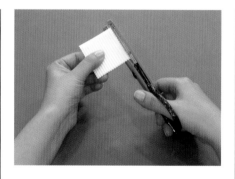

3. Punch out three pale blue flowers. Punch out three yellow circles and attach them to the centers of the flowers.

4. Attach the corrugated board square to the center of the card stock and attach the three pale blue flowers to it.

5. Make four small circles and attach them outside of each outer corner of the white squares.

MATERIALS

white card stock,
  10" x 5" (25 cm x 12.5 cm)
white, pale jade, lavender,
  and purple-pearl paper
butterfly punch
awl
multicircle punch
PVA adhesive
punch wheel
tweezers

Butterflies and White Rectangle

1. Tear by hand three white 1⅕" x 1⅕" (3 cm x 3 cm) squares. Use a punch wheel to add a stitched appearance to the edges.

2. Repeat Step 1 to make three pale jade ⅖" x ⅖" (1 cm x 1 cm) squares. Attach these smaller squares to the centers of the white squares and attach the white squares to white card stock.

3. Punch out three small butterflies and one large butterfly. Attach the small butterflies to the centers of the pale jade squares and the large butterfly to the white card stock.

4. Punch out ten ⅒" (2 mm) circles and attach them in two lines to the white card stock with tweezers.

Friendship

MATERIALS

white card stock,
   10" x 5" (25 cm x 12.5 cm)
fifteen white paper ribbons,
   $\frac{1}{10}$" x 2$\frac{7}{10}$" (2 mm x 5.5 cm)
ten pale blue paper ribbons,
   $\frac{1}{10}$" x 1$\frac{7}{10}$" (2 mm x 4.4 cm)
five pale yellow paper ribbons,
   $\frac{1}{10}$" x 1$\frac{1}{5}$" (2 mm x 3 cm)
foam tape
paper-quilling needle
PVA adhesive
cutting mat
craft knife
tweezers

A Vase and Flowers

1. Make a card using the instructions for Pressing (p. 12).

2. Use the flower pattern on page 95 to cut a flowerpot out of white paper.

3. Make six teardrop petal flowers using white paper ribbons and ten pale blue paper ribbons. (Each flower should have five teardrop petals.) Make tight circles using pale yellow paper ribbons and attach them to the centers of the flowers.

4. Use thin foam tape and tweezers to attach the flowerpot and the five flowers to the front.

5. Make three creeper stems by winding white paper ribbons around a paper-quilling needle and attach them around the flowers.

MATERIALS

white card stock,
  10" x 5" (25 cm x 12.5 cm)
pink and white crinkle paper
yellow, lavender, and jade paper
scissors
circle punch
spray adhesive
PVA adhesive
cutting mat
craft knife
tracing paper
tweezers
"Thank You" characters
  printed on tracing paper

Fence and Flowers

1. Use spray adhesive to attach the "Thank You" tracing paper to the front of the card so that the words are at the bottom center.

2. Cut a 2⅗" x 2⅗" (6.7 cm x 6.7 cm) frame (⅕" [6mm] wide) out of pink crinkle paper. Use an awl to mark lines along the outer edges of the rectangle and fold slightly along the marks to add a three-dimensional effect.

3. Fold lavender paper in half twice and punch out five circles. Fold jade paper in half twice and punch out a circle.

4. Stack four lavender circles together and cut them into a flower petal shape. Add a three-dimensional effect to the petals by curling them slightly with an awl.

5. Attach four petals together to make each flower and attach one yellow circle at the center of each.

6. Use the pattern on page 95 to cut six ⅕" x ½" (5 mm x 1.5 cm) fence posts out of white crinkle paper. Cut them partially up the centers to make them look more natural. Attach the white posts to a thin

1⅘" (4.5 cm)-long white paper strip to complete the fence.

7. Attach the frame to the printed tracing paper with foam tape. Attach the fence, the five flowers, and the leaves in the center of the frame.

8. Punch out a butterfly and attach it inside the frame above the flowers.

MATERIALS

white card stock,
   10" x 5" (25 cm x 12.5 cm)
green, yellow, and red paper
six khaki paper ribbons,
   ¹⁄₁₀" x 3¹⁄₅" (2 mm x 8 cm)
white paper ribbon
foam tape
metal ruler
multicircle punch
PVA adhesive
decorative-edge scissors
cutting mat
craft knife
punch wheel
tweezers

Flowers and Embellishment

1. Attach a red 1³⁄₅" x 1³⁄₅" (4 cm x 4 cm) square to yellow paper and trim the yellow edges with decorative-edge scissors.

2. Use a punch wheel along the outer edges of the red square to create a stitched appearance.

3. Attach the yellow square to a dark green 2" x 2" (5 cm x 5 cm) square with foam tape.

4. Attach the square to the front cover with foam tape.

5. Make one teardrop petal flower using six khaki paper ribbons. Make a tight circle using white paper ribbon and attach it to the center of the flower. Attach the flower to the center of the red square.

6. Punch sixteen ¹⁄₁₀" (2 mm) circles out of yellow paper and attach them in jagged lines to the upper and lower edges of the square.

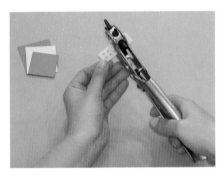

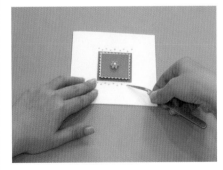

MATERIALS

white card stock,
  10" x 5" (25 cm x 12.5 cm)
yellow, white, gray, blue, purple,
  lavender, and jade paper
flower punch
foam tape
awl
PVA adhesive
tracing paper
punch wheel
tweezers

Butterflies on a Rectangle

1. Tear six ½" x ½" (1.5 cm x 1.5 cm) squares out of yellow paper and use a punch wheel to create a stitched appearance.

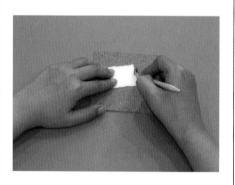

2. Punch six butterflies out of various colored paper and use an awl to poke lines down the centers of them.

3. Attach the butterflies to the squares with foam tape and attach the squares to white card stock in two lines of three squares each.

4. Print "Happy Day" characters on tracing paper with a computer printer. Cut the phrase out and attach it below the squares.

Spring

MATERIALS

white card stock,
   10" x 5" (25 cm x 12.5 cm)
brown crinkle paper
purple, yellow, green,
   and jade paper
butterfly punch
wave-edge scissors
foam tape
awl
metal ruler
stapler
PVA adhesive
cutting mat
craft knife

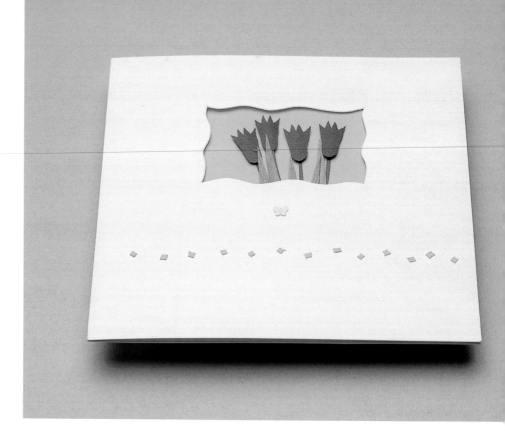

Purple Flowers and a Butterfly

1. Use the window pattern on page 96 to mark with an awl the shape to cut on white card stock.

2. Cut out the rectangle with a craft knife.

3. Cut a rectangle out of yellow paper with wave-edge scissors, making the rectangle ⅖" (1 cm) larger than the window in the card stock. Attach the yellow sheet to the interior card stock.

4. Cut four flowers out of purple paper using the pattern on page 96. Fold the flowers in half slightly to add a three-dimensional effect. Cut stems out of green paper and leaves out of jade crinkle paper.

5. Cut a flower vase out of brown crinkle paper. Slightly fold the vase down the center to add a three-dimensional effect.

6. Attach the purple flowers to the yellow rectangle with foam tape and then attach the stems, the leaves, and the vase.

7. Punch out a butterfly and attach it to the front of the white card stock. Cut fifteen small squares out of yellow paper and attach them to the white card stock in a jagged line.

MATERIALS

white card stock,
10" x 5" (25 cm x 12.5 cm)
pink, pale pink, orange, pale blue, purple, yellow, lavender, dark blue, dark purple, pale green, and dark green paper
scissors
metal ruler
spray adhesive
transparent tape
PVA adhesive
cutting mat
craft knife
tracing paper
tweezers

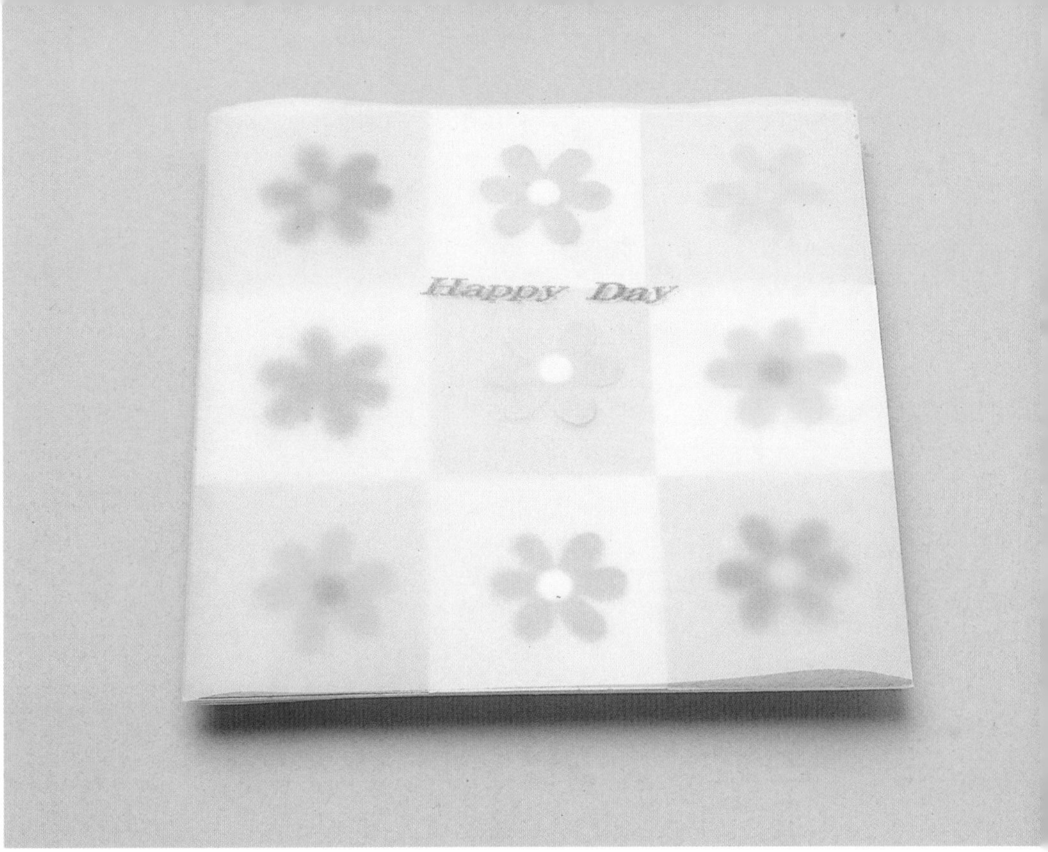

A Bundle of Flowers

1. Print "Happy Day" characters on tracing paper with a computer printer.

2. Stack together pink and pale pink papers. Trisect and cut them vertically and horizontally to make nine 1⅗" x 1⅗" (4.1 cm x 4.1 cm) squares on each paper. Arrange nine of the squares so that the colors alternate and attach them together with transparent tape.

3. Attach the checkered square to white card stock with spray adhesive.

4. Use the pattern on page 96 to cut out one flower each from orange, pale blue, purple, yellow, lavender, dark blue, dark purple, pale green, and dark green paper.

5. Cut out different colored circles and attach them to the centers of flowers.

6. Use tweezers to attach the nine flowers to each of the nine checkered squares on the front of the card.

7. Place the "Happy Day" tracing paper on top of the white card stock with a ⅘" (2 cm) overhang on the left side of the card. Fold the ⅘" (2 cm) overhang and attach it to the back side of the card stock with spray adhesive.

MATERIALS

white card stock,
   10" x 5" (25 cm x 12.5 cm)
yellow, green, pale green,
   orange, and white paper
decorative-edge scissors
foam tape
awl
metal ruler
PVA adhesive
corkboard
cutting mat
craft knife
punch wheel

Yellow Spring Flowers

1. Make a card using the instructions for Pressing (p. 12) and Basic Window-Shaped Card I (p. 13).

2. Stack three pieces of yellow paper and cut out the teardrop pattern on page 96. Do the same once more to make six flower petals in total.

3. Cut a ⅖" (1 cm) circle and attach the flower petals to it with PVA adhesive and tweezers. Cut a ½" (1.5 cm) orange circle and press it slightly with an embossing tool to add a three-dimensional effect.

Attach the circle to the center of the yellow flower. Put the flower on corkboard and use an awl to add stitching around the edges of the center circle and each petal.

4. Make a 2½" x 2½" (6.5 cm x 6.5 cm) square out of green paper and attach it to pale green paper. Trim the pale green paper with decorative-edge scissors.

5. Attach an interior paper between the covers and attach the pale green square to it. Attach the flower to the center of

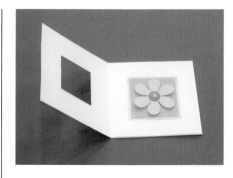

the pale green square with foam tape. Cut out small circles and attach three to the flower center and one to each corner of the green square.

MATERIALS

white card stock,
  10" x 5" (25 cm x 12.5 cm)
white, lavender, and purple paper
tracing pen
two ivory paper ribbons,
  ¹⁄₁₀" x 3⅓" (2 mm x 8 cm)
graph paper
cutting mat
craft knife
foam tape
awl
metal ruler
snowflake punch
multicircle punch
small flower punch
decorative-edge scissors
PVA adhesive
corkboard
punch wheel
tweezers

An Egg Embellished with Flowers

1. Use the pattern on page 96 to cut an egg-shaped window in white card stock. If you want to add a three-dimensional effect to the window, see Pressing (p. 12).

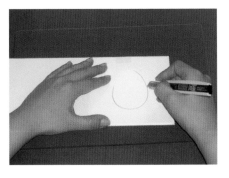

2. Put the egg-shaped piece on a white 3⅓" x 3⅓" (8 cm x 8 cm) square and trace the shape on it. Use decorative-edge scissors to cut out the egg just inside the traced line. Use an awl to poke the lace trim and attach the lace frame to the back side of the front cover.

3. Place a sheet of graph paper ½" (1.5 cm) below the upper line of the white card and mark dots with a ⅕" (5 mm) gap. Slide the graph paper down to create another row of dots offset from the first. Add a three-dimensional effect by pressing the opposite side of it with a tracing pen.

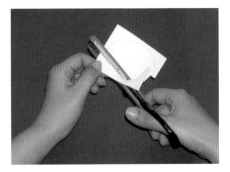

4. Use foam tape to attach a white 3⁹⁄₁₀" x 3⅕" (10 cm x 8 cm) rectangle behind the lace frame on the back side of the front cover.

5. Place two ivory paper ribbons on corkboard and roll a punch wheel up the center. Attach the ribbons in a cross shape at the center of the egg-shaped hole.

6. Punch out two snowflakes and stack them so they do not line up evenly. Punch out eight small flowers and attach them around the snowflake in the egg-shaped window.

Thank You

Summer, Autumn, Winter

Happy Days

MATERIALS

white card stock,
  10" x 5" (25 cm x 12.5 cm)
pale green, white, and
  yellow paper
scissors
paper crimper
flower stencil pattern
circle punch
foam tape
metal ruler
PVA adhesive
cutting mat
craft knife

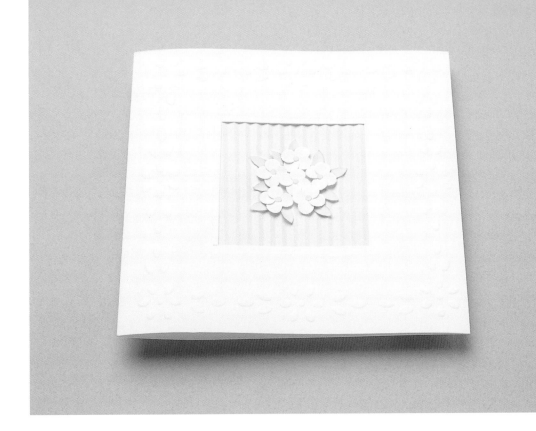

Cute White Flowers

1. Make a card using the instructions for Pressing (p. 12) and Basic Window-Shaped Card I (p. 13).

2. Put pale green paper through a paper crimper to make a corrugated effect on the surface and cut it into a 3⅕" x 3⅕" (8 cm x 8 cm) square.

3. Fold white paper in half twice and punch out a circle. Attach the four resulting circles together to make a white flower. Attach a small yellow circle at the center of the flower. Make five more flowers in the same manner.

4. Fold the yellow paper in half and cut out ten leaves.

5. Attach the pale green square to the back side of the front cover.

6. Attach one white flower to the center of the pale green square with foam tape and attach the other five flowers around the center flower. Attach the leaves around the flowers.

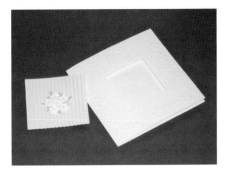

MATERIALS

white card stock,
  10" x 5" (25 cm x 12.5 cm)
white and yellow paper
scissors
PVA adhesive
cutting mat
craft knife
punch wheel
stapler

Yellow Flowers Behind a Window

1. Make a card using the instructions for Basic Window-Shaped Card III (p. 15). Attach tracing paper to the back side of the front cover.

2. Stack four pieces of white paper together, with the square and flower pattern from page 97 on top. Use a craft knife to cut the flowers out of the paper and then cut along the edges of the square. You should end up with four 1⅓" x 1⅓" (3 cm x 3 cm) squares with empty flower shapes in the centers.

3. Use a punch wheel along the outer edges of the squares and attach yellow paper to the back sides of the squares with PVA adhesive. Cut out four white circles and attach them to the centers of the flowers.

4. Attach the four squares to the interior paper with PVA adhesive, making sure they line up with the windows in the front cover.

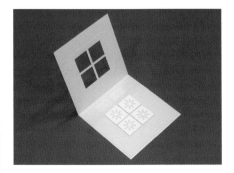

MATERIALS

white card stock,
  10" x 5" (25 cm x 12.5 cm)
white, bright green, lavender,
  yellow, pale blue, jade, and
  purple paper
flower punch
circle punch
foam tape
metal ruler
PVA adhesive
cutting mat
craft knife
tweezers

Flowers and Waves

1. Make a card using the instructions for Pressing (p. 12).

2. Copy the wave pattern on page 97 and place it on white paper. Use a craft knife to cut out the squares and the waves within each one.

3. Make two 1" x 1" (2.5 cm x 2.5 cm) squares out of lavender and bright green paper and attach the squares to the back sides of the wave squares.

4. Punch four flowers out of the lavender, yellow, pale blue, jade, and purple paper. Attach the flowers to the centers of the wave squares.

5. Attach the wave squares to the front cover with foam tape.

MATERIALS

white card stock,
  10" x 5" (25 cm x 12.5 cm)
pale pink, pale blue, lavender,
  dark jade, and jade-pearl paper
five white paper ribbons,
  ¹⁄₁₀" x 1⅘" (2 mm x 4.5 cm)
metal ruler
stapler
PVA adhesive
cutting mat
craft knife
corkboard
punch wheel
awl

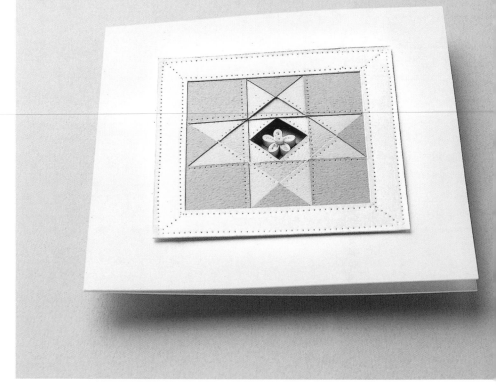

Patterns and Flowers I

1. Cut a 1⅕" x 1⅕" (3 cm x 3 cm) diamond out of white card stock.

2. Cut 3⁹⁄₁₀" x 3⁹⁄₁₀" (10 cm x 10 cm) squares out of pale pink, lavender, pale blue, and dark jade paper.

3. Make four copies of the quilt pattern on page 97 and attach it to each of the squares with a stapler. On the pale pink paper, use an awl to mark the points of the ½" x ½" (1.5 cm x 1.5 cm) diamond in the center of the pattern. On the purple paper, mark the points of the ⅖" x ⅖"

(2 cm x 2 cm) square around the center diamond. On the pale blue paper, mark the points of the 1⅕" x 1⅕" (3 cm x 3 cm) diamond. On the dark jade paper, mark the points of the outer cross shape with the fish-tailed ends.

4. Remove the patterns and use a craft knife to cut the shapes out of each paper.

5. Layer the frames created in Step 4 starting with the pale pink frame and continuing each layer with the next largest shape. Use a punch wheel around the edges of each shape.

6. Cut a 3³⁄₁₀" x 3³⁄₁₀" (8.5 cm x 8.5 cm) frame (⅖" [1 cm] wide) out of jade-pearl and attach the frame on top of the completed piece made in Step 5.

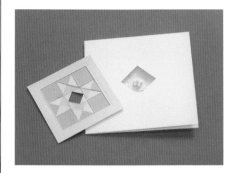

7. Attach the completed frame to the white card stock so that the pale pink cutout diamond is centered in the diamond cut out in Step 1.

8. Make a white teardrop petal flower using five white paper ribbons. Attach the flower to the interior page in the center of the diamond window.

MATERIALS

white card stock,
   10" x 5" (25 cm x 12.5 cm)
gray, jade, white, and
   pale green paper
thick white paper
flower punch
foam tape
metal ruler
multicircle punch
PVA adhesive
cutting mat
craft knife
punch wheel
tweezers

White Flowers on a Rectangle

1. Cut a 2¼" x 5" (6 cm x 12.5 cm) rectangle out of gray paper and attach to a piece of thick white paper of the same size. Use a multicircle punch to make a hole at a point ½" (1.5 cm) below the top edge and 1⅕" (3 cm) from the right edge. Make three other holes using the same measurements on the other edges of the rectangle. (See the pattern on page 97.)

2. Put the rectangle on a cutting mat and cut curved lines between the two holes on the top and the two holes on the bottom. Use a punch wheel to create a stitched appearance just above the top curved line and just below the bottom line.

3. Cut a 2¼" x 2¼" (6 cm x 6 cm) square out of jade paper and roll a punch wheel along the outer edges. Slide two corners of the square through the curved lines in the rectangle so the jade square is positioned as a diamond.

4. Punch out six large flowers. Attach two pieces together to make three flowers. Attach the flowers in a line to the center of the jade diamond. Make five ¹⁄₁₀" (2 mm) circles with a multicircle punch and attach them in a line above the flowers.

5. Print "Happy Days" characters with a computer printer. Use an awl to mark a rectangle around the phrase, roll a punch wheel over the lines, and then tear along the lines. Attach the rectangle below the flowers.

MATERIALS

white card stock,
  10" x 5" (25 cm x 12.5 cm)
red paper
twelve pink paper ribbons,
  ¹⁄₁₀" x 4¾" (2 mm x 12 cm)
six pale pink paper ribbons,
  ¹⁄₁₀" x 4¾" (2 mm x 12 cm)
three white paper ribbons,
  ¹⁄₁₀" x 2" (2 mm x 5 cm)
foam tape
awl
metal ruler
PVA adhesive
cutting mat
craft knife
corkboard
punch wheel
heart punch

Three Paper-Quilling Flowers

1. Make a card using the instructions for Basic Card II (p. 10).

2. Cut three 1¹⁄₁₀" x 1¹⁄₁₀" (2.7 cm x 2.7 cm) squares out of red paper. Place the squares on corkboard and roll a punch wheel along the outer edges.

3. Make marquise petal flowers using seven pale pink paper ribbons and fourteen pink paper ribbons. Make tight circles using three white paper ribbons and attach them to the centers of the flowers.

4. Use foam tape to attach the left sides of the red squares to the left flap of the front cover. (The right sides of the squares will overlap the right flap of the cover.)

5. Attach flowers to the red squares. Punch six hearts out of pale pink paper and attach them in two vertical rows on the right and left flaps.

MATERIALS

jade card stock,
  10" x 5" (25 cm x 12.5 cm)
jade crinkle paper
orange, dark green, lavender,
  pale green, jade, and pale
  blue paper
gold gel pen
snowflake punch
foam tape
metal ruler
multicircle punch
decorative-edge scissors
PVA adhesive
punch wheel
tweezers

Patterns

1. Cut four 1" x 1" (2.5 cm x 2.5 cm) squares out of jade crinkle paper and roll a punch wheel along the edges.

2. Attach the jade squares to orange paper and use decorative-edge scissors to trim the orange paper, leaving a ¹⁄₂₀" (1 mm) margin. Attach the orange squares to dark green 1⅕" x 1⅕" (3 cm x 3 cm) squares with foam tape.

3. Punch two snowflakes out of lavender, pale blue, and jade paper and attach the matching color snowflakes together with

foam tape. Cut out four yellow circles and attach them to the centers of the snowflakes.

4. Attach the snowflakes to the jade squares and attach the completed squares to the white card stock. Use the gold gel pen to write a signature or message below the squares.

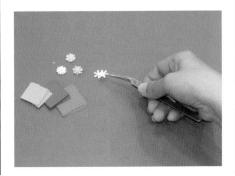

MATERIALS

jade card stock with
  embellished surface,
  10" x 5" (25 cm x 12.5 cm)
pale jade rice paper
white and pale yellow paper
four ivory paper ribbons,
  1/10" x 2½" (2 mm x 6.5 cm)
foam tape
spray adhesive
metal ruler
small flower punch
PVA adhesive
cutting mat
craft knife
corkboard
large flower punch
punch wheel
tweezers

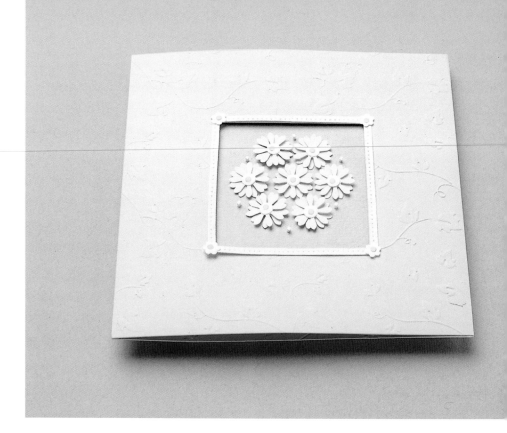

Daisy

1. Make a card using the instructions for Basic Window-Shaped Card I (p. 13).

2. Place four ivory paper ribbons on corkboard and roll a punch wheel up the center. Attach the ribbons to the edges of the window, overlapping each other at the corners.

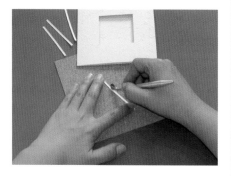

3. Punch out four white flowers with a small flower punch and attach them to the corners where the ribbons meet.

4. Punch out fourteen white flowers with a large flower punch. Attach two flowers together with foam tape and add white and yellow circles to the center to make a daisy. Repeat this process for a total of seven daisies.

5. Apply spray adhesive to the back side of the front cover and attach a 3 9/10" x 3 9/10" (10 cm x 10 cm) square of pale jade rice paper.

6. Attach one daisy to the center of the square window and arrange the other six daisies around it.

7. Place white paper on foam tape and cut small rectangles out of it. Attach the small rectangles between the six outer daisies.

MATERIALS

white card stock,
  10" x 5" (25 cm x 12.5 cm)
thick white paper
lavender paper
tracing paper
white translucent fabric ribbon,
  3⅕" x 2¼" (8 cm x 6 cm)
star punch
metal ruler
spray adhesive
PVA adhesive
cutting mat
craft knife

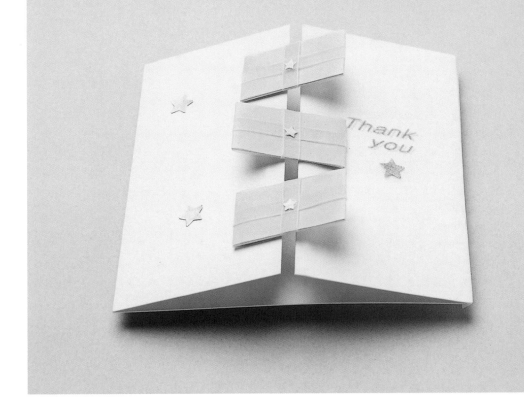

A Wrapped Gift Box

1. Make a card using the instructions for Basic Card II (p. 10).

2. Print "Thank you" characters with a computer printer and use spray adhesive to attach it to the right flap of the card cover.

3. Attach lavender paper to thick white paper and cut three 1¹⁄₁₀" x 1⅗" (2.7 cm x 4 cm) rectangles out of it.

4. Attach 1¹⁄₁₀" x 2¾" (2.7 cm x 7 cm) tracing paper rectangles to the lavender

rectangles so that there is a ¹⁄₂₀" (1 mm) margin on each end. Fold the margins and attach them to the back side of the lavender rectangles.

5. Use PVA adhesive to attach white fabric ribbon horizontally and vertically to the lavender rectangles. Punch out stars and attach them to the center points where the ribbons overlap.

6. Attach the right side of one rectangle to the right cover flap. Attach the left sides of the other rectangles to the left cover flap above and below the center rectangle.

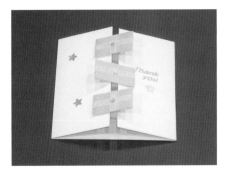

MATERIALS

white card stock,
   10" x 5" (25 cm x 12.5 cm)
thick white paper
bright green and lavender paper
four white paper ribbons,
   ⅕" x 4¾" (6 mm x 12 cm)
four bright green paper ribbons,
   ¹⁄₁₀" x 4¾" (2 mm x 12 cm)
metal ruler
butterfly punch
yellow highlighter
PVA adhesive
cutting mat
craft knife

Butterflies and a Frame II

1. Print the "Thank you" characters on tracing paper with a computer printer.

2. Attach one bright green paper ribbon to each of the white paper ribbons, then attach the four ribbons along the outer edges of white card stock with PVA adhesive.

3. Attach bright green paper to thick white paper and cut a 2½" x 2½" (6.5 cm x 6.5 cm) square out of it. Cut a smaller 1⅕" x 1⅕" (3 cm x 3 cm) square from the 2½" x 2½" (6.5 cm x 6.5 cm) square.

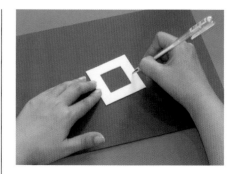

4. Use a yellow highlighter to make dots on the bright green frame. Cut a 2½" x 2½" (6.5 cm x 6.5 cm) square around the "Thank You" characters and attach it on top of the frame.

5. Punch out two butterflies and attach one to the upper part of the frame and one to the lower part of it.

MATERIALS

white card stock,
  10" x 5" (25 cm x 12.5 cm)
gold, pale green, and
  dark green paper
twenty-six white paper ribbons,
  1/10" x 4¾" (2 mm x 12 cm)
one pale green paper ribbon,
  1/10" x 1⅕" (2 mm x 3 cm)
gold gel pen
foam tape
metal ruler
small flower punch
cutting mat
craft knife

A White Flower in a Frame

1. Cut a 1⅖" x 1⅖" (3.5 cm x 3.5 cm) square out of a dark green 2½" x 2½" (6.5 cm x 6.5 cm) square to create a frame. Attach it to a gold ⅕" x 3" (5 mm x 7.5 cm) rectangle.

2. Trim the gold paper from the center of the frame, leaving a 1/10" (2 mm) margin.

3. Write "Happy Day" with a gold gel pen on each side of the frame.

4. Make a teardrop petal flower using white paper ribbons.

5. Use foam tape to attach the frame to the center of white card stock and attach the paper-quilling flower to the center of the frame. Make a tight circle using pale green paper ribbon and attach it to the center of the white flower.

6. Punch four small flowers out of dark green paper. Cut small circles out of pale green paper and attach them to the centers of the punched flowers. Attach the flowers to the frame.

MATERIALS

pale jade card stock,
   10" x 5" (25 cm x 12.5 cm)
pink and jade crinkle paper
thick white paper
six pale green ribbons,
   ¹⁄₁₀" x 2⁷⁄₁₀" (2 mm x 5.5 cm)
one white paper ribbon,
   ¹⁄₁₀" x 1¹⁄₅" (2 mm x 3 cm)
awl
metal ruler
multicircle punch
stapler
spray adhesive
cutting mat
craft knife
punch wheel
corkboard
tweezers

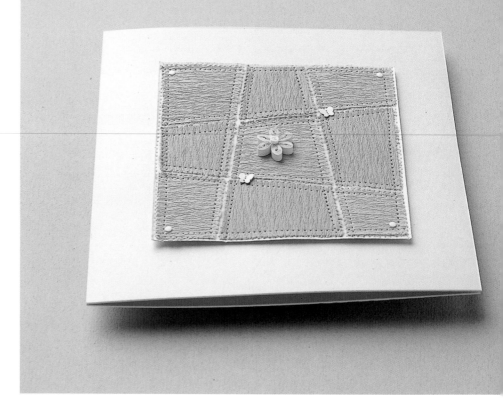

Patterns and Flowers II

1. Cut a 3³⁄₁₀" x 3³⁄₁₀" (8.5 cm x 8.5 cm) square out of thick white paper.

2. Attach 4¾" x 4¾" (12 cm x 12 cm) pink crinkle paper and 4¾" x 4¾" (12 cm x 12 cm) jade crinkle paper with a stapler. Place the pattern on page 97 on top of the papers. Use an awl to mark the points of the trapezoids.

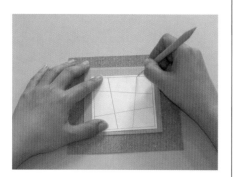

3. Remove the pattern and use an awl to mark the lines between the points marked on the pink crinkle paper. Do the same on the jade crinkle paper.

4. Place the crinkle paper on corkboard and roll a punch wheel along all the marked lines. Tear off by hand the nine segments of the crinkle paper. Place the shapes down in the same order.

5. Attach the pink and jade pieces to a white 3³⁄₁₀" x 3³⁄₁₀" (8.5 cm x 8.5 cm) square with tweezers, but arrange them so that the same color pieces are not next to each other.

6. Roll a punch wheel along the edges of each piece to add stitching.

7. Make a teardrop petal flower using six pale green paper ribbons. Make a tight circle using a white paper ribbon and attach it to the center of the flower.

8. Use foam tape to attach the quilted square to the center of the white card stock and attach the flower to the center of the quilted square.

9. Punch out four circles and attach them to the corners of the quilted square.

10. Punch out two butterflies and attach them to the quilted square.

⤋ P. 15 | BASIC WINDOW-SHAPED CARD III

⤋ P. 16 | BASIC WINDOW-SHAPED CARD IV

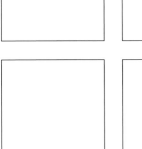

➜ P. 17 | BASIC EMBOSSING

⬇ **P. 21 | TRADITIONAL**
     PATTERN CARD III

⬇ **P. 26 | WINE GLASSES IN A FRAME**

⬇ **P. 27 | WINE GLASSES**

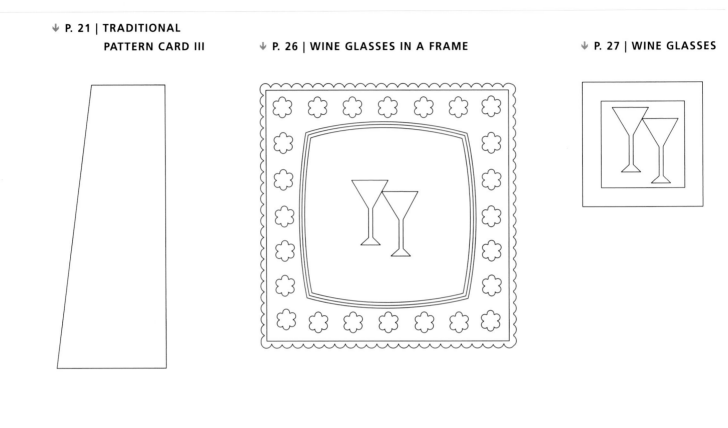

⬇ **P. 28 | CAKE AND HEART**

➡ **P. 29 | ANNIVERSARY CAKE**

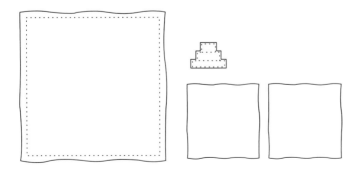

← P. 32 | CARNATION AND LACE HEART

Happy   Mother's Day

↓ P. 33 | PURPLE FLOWERS AND FLOWER VASE

I

HAPPY

YOU

↗ P. 39 | SILVER AND RED HEART

↘ P. 42 | FORK AND KNIFE

↓ P. 43 | A RED ROOF

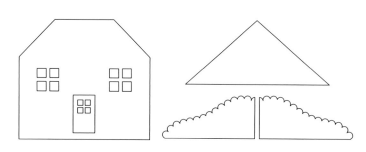

↘ P. 44 | A COFFE MUG

↓ P. 46 | FLOWERS IN A FRAME

↘ P. 47 | EMBOSSED FLOWERS AND HAPPY BIRTHDAY

↓ P. 49 | CARD EMBELLISHED WITH FLOWERS

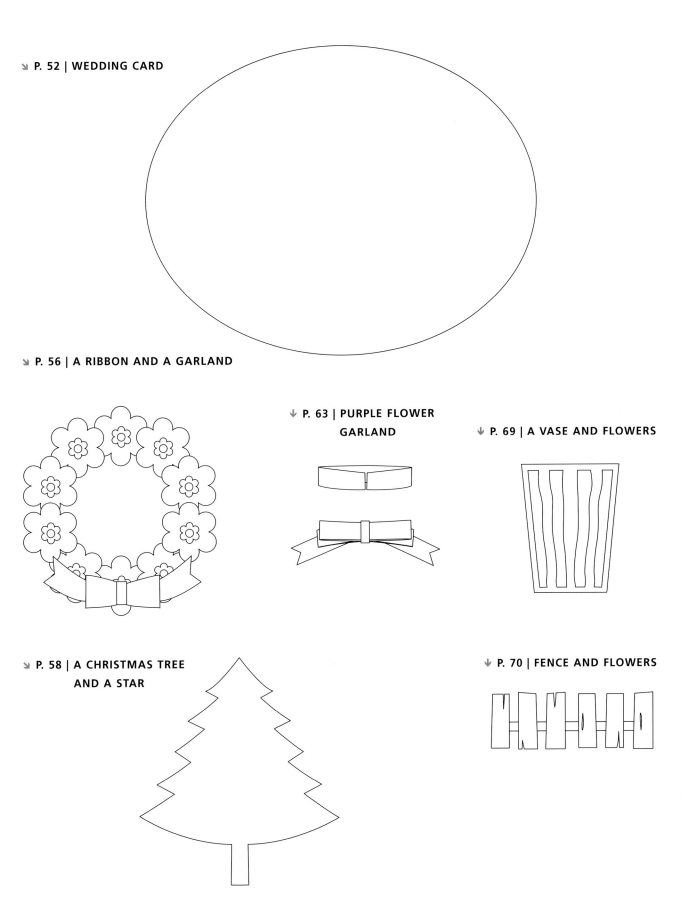

↘ P. 52 | WEDDING CARD

↘ P. 56 | A RIBBON AND A GARLAND

↓ P. 63 | PURPLE FLOWER
GARLAND

↓ P. 69 | A VASE AND FLOWERS

↘ P. 58 | A CHRISTMAS TREE
AND A STAR

↓ P. 70 | FENCE AND FLOWERS

↓ P. 74 | PURPLE FLOWERS AND A BUTTERFLY

↓ P. 75 | A BUNDLE OF FLOWERS

↙ P. 76 | YELLOW SPRING FLOWERS

↘ P. 77 | AN EGG EMBELLISHED WITH FLOWERS

↘ **P. 80 | YELLOW FLOWERS BEHIND A WINDOW**

→ **P. 81 | FLOWERS AND WAVES**

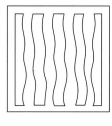

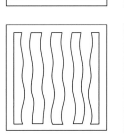

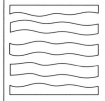

↓ **P. 83 | WHITE FLOWERS ON A RECTANGLE**

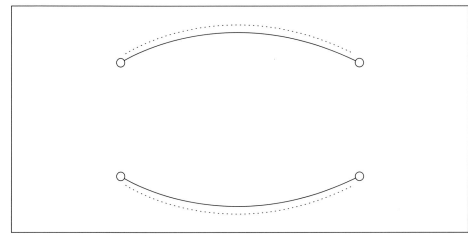

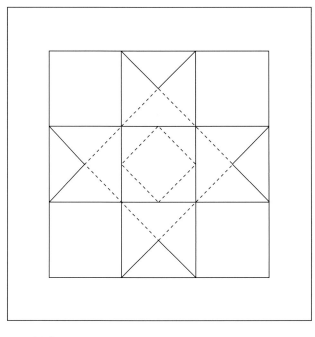

↑ **P. 82 | PATTERNS AND FLOWERS I**

↑ **P. 90 | PATTERNS AND FLOWERS II**